A Practical English Grammar
Exercises 1

Third edition

A Practical English Grammar
Exercises 1

A. J. Thomson
A. V. Martinet

Oxford University Press

OXFORD
UNIVERSITY PRESS

Great Clarendon Street, Oxford OX2 6DP

Oxford University Press is a department of the University of Oxford.
It furthers the University's objective of excellence in research, scholarship,
and education by publishing worldwide in

Oxford New York

Auckland Cape Town Dar es Salaam Hong Kong Karachi
Kuala Lumpur Madrid Melbourne Mexico City Nairobi
New Delhi Shanghai Taipei Toronto

With offices in

Argentina Austria Brazil Chile Czech Republic France Greece
Guatemala Hungary Italy Japan Poland Portugal Singapore
South Korea Switzerland Thailand Turkey Ukraine Vietnam

OXFORD and OXFORD ENGLISH are registered trade marks of
Oxford University Press in the UK and in certain other countries

ISBN-13: 978 0 19 431343 8

Typeset in Great Britain by VAP Group, Kidlington, Oxford

Printed in China

Preface to the third edition

This is one of two books of exercises designed to accompany
A Practical English Grammar.

To coincide with the publication of the fourth edition of the
Grammar the books have been altered in the following ways:

1 Some exercises have been transferred from Book 1 to Book 2
and some from Book 2 to Book 1. Where exercises on similar
structures appear in both books, those in Book 2 are slightly
more difficult than those in Book 1.

2 The sequence of the exercises in both books has been
rearranged to conform to the order of chapters in the *Grammar.*

3 Four exercises have been added to Book 1, bringing the total to
100, and one to Book 2, bringing the total to 90.

4 Changes have been made to the text of some of the exercises,
chiefly in Book 1.

5 The grading of the exercises has now been extended to both
books. ■ means difficult, ◪ means moderately difficult and
□ means easy. The gradings are printed at the head of each
exercise.

6 The numbers printed after 'PEG' at the head of each exercise
now refer to paragraphs in the fourth edition of the *Grammar.*

Answers have been supplied to most of the exercises. They are to
be found in the key at the end of each book.

Some of the exercises are in the form of a dialogue between two
people. Where the speakers are not named, a change of speaker is
shown by the symbol ' ~ '.

Contents

Contents

3 Present and past tenses
PEG chapters 17–18

4 Future forms
PEG chapter 19

5 Conditionals
PEG chapter 21

6 Infinitive
PEG chapter 23

7 Gerund, infinitive and participles
PEG chapters 23–6

8 Passive
PEG chapter 30

Contents

9 Indirect speech

PEG chapter 31

10 Purpose

PEG chapter 33

Key

1 Articles

1 Articles: a/an

☑ PEG 1–4

Insert **a** or **an** if necessary.

1 My neighbour is . . . photographer; let's ask him for . . . advice about colour films.
2 We had . . . fish and . . . chips for . . . lunch. ~
   That doesn't sound . . . very interesting lunch.
3 I had . . . very bad night; I didn't sleep . . . wink.
4 He is . . . vegetarian; you won't get . . . meat at his house. He'll give you . . . nut cutlet. ~
   Last time I had . . . nut cutlet I had . . . indigestion.
5 . . . travel agent would give you . . . information about . . . hotels.
6 We'd better go by . . . taxi—if we can get . . . taxi at such . . . hour as 2 a.m.
7 . . . person who suffers from . . . claustrophobia has . . . dread of being confined in . . . small space, and would always prefer . . . stairs to . . . lift.
8 Do you take . . . sugar in . . . coffee? ~
   I used to, but now I'm on . . . diet. I'm trying to lose . . . weight.
9 . . . man suffering from . . . shock should not be given anything to drink.
10 You'll get . . . shock if you touch . . . live wire with that screwdriver. Why don't you get . . . screwdriver with . . . insulated handle?
11 It costs fifty-five and . . . half pence and I've only got . . . fifty pence piece. ~
   You can pay by . . . cheque here. ~
   But can I write . . . cheque for . . . fifty-five and . . . half pence?
12 . . . Mr Smith is . . . old customer and . . . honest man. ~
   Why do you say that? Has he been accused of . . . dishonesty?
13 I'm not . . . wage-earner; I'm . . . self-employed man. I have . . . business of my own. ~
   Then you're not . . . worker; you're . . . capitalist!
14 When he was charged with . . . murder he said he had . . . alibi.
15 . . . friend of mine is expecting . . . baby. If it's . . . girl she's going to be called Etheldreda. ~
   What . . . name to give . . . girl!

16 I have . . . hour and . . . half for lunch. ~
I only have . . . half . . . hour—barely . . . time for . . . smoke and . . . cup of coffee.

17 I hope you have . . . lovely time and . . . good weather. ~
But I'm not going for . . . holiday; I'm going on . . . business.

18 He looked at me with . . . horror when I explained that I was . . . double agent.

19 I wouldn't climb . . . mountain for £1,000! I have . . . horror of . . . heights.

20 I have . . . headache and . . . sore throat. I think I've got . . . cold. ~
I think you're getting . . . flu.

21 . . . Mr Jones called while you were out (*neither of us knows this man*). He wants to make . . . complaint about . . . article in the paper. He was in . . . very bad temper.

22 If you go by . . . train you can have quite . . . comfortable journey, but make sure you get . . . express, not . . . train that stops at all the stations.

23 . . . few people know (*hardly anyone knows*) that there is . . . secret passage from this house to . . . old smugglers' cave in the cliffs.

24 I'm having . . . few friends in to . . . coffee tomorrow evening. Would you like to come? ~
I'd love to, but I'm afraid I'm going to . . . concert.

25 It's time you had . . . holiday. You haven't had . . . day off for . . . month.

26 He broke . . . leg in . . . skiing accident. It's still in . . . plaster.

27 I want . . . assistant with . . . knowledge of French and . . . experience of . . . office routine.

28 I see that your house is built of . . . wood. Are you insured against . . . fire?

29 The escaping prisoner camped in . . . wood but he didn't light . . . fire because . . . smoke rising from the wood might attract . . . attention.

30 I had . . . amazing experience last night. I saw . . . dinosaur eating . . . meat pie in . . . London park. ~
You mean you had . . . nightmare. Anyway, dinosaurs didn't eat . . . meat.

31 I'll pay you . . . hundred . . . week. It's not . . . enormous salary but after all you are . . . completely unskilled man.

32 If you kept . . . graph you could see at . . . glance whether you were making . . . profit or . . . loss.

33 . . . little (*hardly anything*) is known about the effect of this drug; yet . . . chemist will sell it to you without . . . prescription.

34 I have . . . little money left; let's have dinner in . . . restaurant.

35 Would it be . . . trouble to you to buy me . . . newspaper on your way home?

36 . . . man is . . . reasoning animal.

2 Articles: the

◢ PEG 6-8

Insert **the** if necessary.

1 . . . youngest boy has just started going to . . . school; . . . eldest boy is at . . . college.
2 She lives on . . . top floor of an old house. When . . . wind blows, all . . . windows rattle.
3 . . . darkness doesn't worry . . . cats; . . . cats can see in . . . dark.
4 My little boys say that they want to be . . . spacemen, but most of them will probably end up in . . . less dramatic jobs.
5 Do you know . . . time? ~
   Yes, . . . clock in . . . hall has just struck nine. ~
   Then it isn't . . . time to go yet.
6 He was sent to . . . prison for . . . six months for . . . shop-lifting. When . . . six months are over he'll be released; . . . difficulty then will be to find . . . work. ~
   Do you go to . . . prison to visit him?
7 I went to . . . school to talk to . . . headmistress. I persuaded her to let Ann give up . . . gymnastics and take . . . ballet lessons instead.
8 . . . ballet isn't much use for . . . girls; it is much better to be able to play . . . piano.
9 I am on . . . night duty. When you go to . . . bed, I go to . . . work.
10 Peter's at . . . office but you could get him on . . . phone. There's a telephone box just round . . . corner
11 He got . . . bronchitis and was taken to . . . hospital. I expect they'll send him home at . . . end of . . . week. ~
   Have you rung . . . hospital to ask how he is?
12 Ann's habit of riding a motorcycle up and down . . . road early in . . . morning annoyed . . . neighbours and in . . . end they took her to . . . court.
13 He first went to . . . sea in a Swedish ship, so as well as learning . . . navigation he had to learn . . . Swedish.
14 . . . family hotels are . . . hotels which welcome . . . parents and . . . children.
15 On . . . Sundays my father stays in . . . bed till ten o'clock, reading . . . Sunday papers.
16 Then he gets up, puts on . . . old clothes, has . . . breakfast and starts . . . work in . . . garden.
17 My mother goes to . . . church in . . . morning, and in . . . afternoon goes to visit . . . friends.
18 Like many women, she loves . . . tea parties and . . . gossip.
19 My parents have . . . cold meat and . . . salad for . . . supper, . . . winter and . . . summer.
20 During . . . meal he talks about . . . garden and she tells him . . . village gossip.

21 We have a very good train service from here to . . . city centre and most people go to . . . work by train. You can go by . . . bus too, of course, but you can't get a season ticket on . . . bus.

22 . . . dead no longer need . . . help. We must concern ourselves with . . . living. We must build . . . houses and . . . schools and . . . playgrounds.

23 I'd like to see . . . Mr Smith please. ~
Do you mean . . . Mr Smith who works in . . . box office or . . . other Mr Smith?

24 Did you come by . . . air? ~
No, I came by . . . sea. I had a lovely voyage on . . . Queen Elizabeth II.

25 . . . most of . . . stories that . . . people tell about . . . Irish aren't true.

26 . . . married couples with . . . children often rent . . . cottages by . . . seaside for . . . summer holidays.
. . . men hire boats and go for . . . trips along . . . coast; . . . children spend . . . day on . . . beach and . . . poor mothers spend . . . most of . . . time doing . . . cooking and cleaning.

27 It's usually safe to walk on . . . sand, but here, when . . . tide is coming in, . . . sand becomes dangerously soft. . . . people have been swallowed up by it.

28 When . . . Titanic was crossing . . . Atlantic she struck an iceberg which tore a huge hole in her bow. . . . captain ordered . . . crew to help . . . passengers into . . . boats.

29 Everywhere . . . man has cut down . . . forests in order to cultivate . . . ground, or to use . . . wood as . . . fuel or as . . . building material.

30 But . . . interference with . . . nature often brings . . . disaster. . . . tree-felling sometimes turns . . . fertile land into a dustbowl.

31 . . . people think that . . . lead is . . . heaviest metal, but . . . gold is heavier.

32 Our air hostess said, '. . . rack is only for . . . light articles. . . . heavy things such as . . . bottles must be put on . . . floor.'

33 . . . windows are supposed to let in . . . light; but . . . windows of this house are so small that we have to have . . . electric light on all . . . time.

34 There'll always be a conflict between . . . old and . . . young. . . . young people want . . . change but . . . old people want . . . things to stay . . . same.

35 . . . power tends to corrupt and . . . absolute power corrupts absolutely.

36 You can fool some of . . . people all . . . time, and all . . . people some of . . . time; but you cannot fool all . . . people all . . . time.

3 Articles: a/an, the

■ PEG 1–8

Insert **a, an** or **the** if necessary.

1 There was . . . knock on . . . door. I opened it and found . . . small dark man in . . . blue overcoat and . . . woollen cap.
2 He said he was . . . employee of . . . gas company and had come to read . . . meter.
3 But I had . . . suspicion that he wasn't speaking . . . truth because . . . meter readers usually wear . . . peaked caps.
4 However, I took him to . . . meter, which is in . . . dark corner under . . . stairs (. . . meters are usually in . . . dark corners under . . . stairs).
5 I asked if he had . . . torch; he said he disliked torches and always read . . . meters by . . . light of . . . match.
6 I remarked that if there was . . . leak in . . . gaspipe there might be . . . explosion while he was reading . . . meter.
7 He said, 'As . . . matter of . . . fact, there was . . . explosion in . . . last house I visited; and Mr Smith, . . . owner of . . . house, was burnt in . . . face.'
8 'Mr Smith was holding . . . lighted match at . . . time of . . . explosion.'
9 To prevent . . . possible repetition of this accident, I lent him . . . torch.
10 He switched on . . . torch, read . . . meter and wrote . . . reading down on . . . back of . . . envelope.
11 I said in . . . surprise that . . . meter readers usually put . . . readings down in . . . book.
12 He said that he had had . . . book but that it had been burnt in . . . fire in . . . Mr Smith's house.
13 By this time I had come to . . . conclusion that he wasn't . . . genuine meter reader; and . . . moment he left . . . house I rang . . . police.
14 Are John and Mary . . . cousins? ~
   No, they aren't . . . cousins; they are . . . brother and . . . sister.
15 . . . fog was so thick that we couldn't see . . . side of . . . road. We followed . . . car in front of us and hoped that we were going . . . right way.
16 I can't remember . . . exact date of . . . storm, but I know it was . . . Sunday because everybody was at . . . church. On . . . Monday . . . post didn't come because . . . roads were blocked by . . . fallen trees.
17 Peter thinks that this is quite . . . cheap restaurant.
18 There's been . . . murder here. ~
   Where's . . . body? ~
   There isn't . . . body. ~
   Then how do you know there's been . . . murder?

Articles

19 Number . . . hundred and two, . . . house next door to us, is for sale. It's quite . . . nice house with . . . big rooms. . . . back windows look out on . . . park.

20 I don't know what . . . price . . . owners are asking. But Dry and Rot are . . . agents. You could give them . . . ring and make them . . . offer.

21 . . . postman's little boy says that he'd rather be . . . dentist than . . . doctor, because . . . dentists don't get called out at . . . night.

22 Just as . . . air hostess (*there was only one on the plane*) was handing me . . . cup of . . . coffee . . . plane gave . . . lurch and . . . coffee went all over . . . person on . . . other side of . . . gangway.

23 There was . . . collision between . . . car and . . . cyclist at . . . crossroads near . . . my house early in . . . morning. . . . cyclist was taken to . . . hospital with . . . concussion. . . . driver of . . . car was treated for . . . shock. . . . witnesses say that . . . car was going at . . . seventy miles . . . hour.

24 Professor Jones, . . . man who discovered . . . new drug that everyone is talking about, refused to give . . . press conference.

25 Peter Piper, . . . student in . . . professor's college, asked him why he refused to talk to . . . press.

26 We're going to . . . tea with . . . Smiths today, aren't we? Shall we take . . . car? ~
We can go by . . . car if you wash . . . car first. We can't go to . . . Mrs Smith's in . . . car all covered with . . . mud.

27 He got . . . job in . . . south and spent . . . next two years doing . . . work he really enjoyed.

28 It is . . . pleasure to do . . . business with such . . . efficient organization.

29 . . . day after . . . day passed without . . . news, and we began to lose . . . hope.

30 Would you like to hear . . . story about . . . Englishman, . . . Irishman and . . . Scotsman? ~
No. I've heard . . . stories about . . . Englishmen, . . . Irishmen and . . . Scotsmen before and they are all . . . same.

31 But mine is not . . . typical story. In my story . . . Scotsman is generous, . . . Irishman is logical and . . . Englishman is romantic. ~
Oh, if it's . . . fantastic story I'll listen with . . . pleasure.

32 My aunt lived on . . . ground floor of . . . old house on . . . River Thames. She was very much afraid of . . . burglars and always locked up . . . house very carefully before she went to . . . bed. She also took . . . precaution of looking under . . . bed to see if . . . burglar was hiding there.

33 '. . . modern burglars don't hide under . . . beds,' said her daughter. 'I'll go on looking just . . . same,' said my aunt.

34 One morning she rang her daughter in . . . triumph. 'I found . . . burglar under . . . bed . . . last night,' she said, 'and he was quite . . . young man.'

35 . . . apples are sold by . . . pound. These are forty pence . . . pound.
36 It was . . . windy morning but they hired . . . boat and went for . . .
sail along . . . coast. In . . . afternoon . . . wind increased and they
soon found themselves in . . . difficulties.

4 Articles and possessive adjectives

☑ PEG 1–8, 62–3

Insert **a, an, the,** or **my, his, her, our, your, their** if necessary.

1 He took off . . . coat and set to work.
2 Why are you standing there with . . . hands in . . . pockets?
3 At most meetings . . . people vote by raising . . . right hands.
4 The bullet struck him in . . . foot.
5 They tied . . . hands behind . . . back and locked him in a cellar.
6 He took . . . shoes off and entered on . . . tiptoe.
7 Someone threw . . . egg which struck the speaker on . . . shoulder.
8 I have . . . headache.
9 I have . . . pain in . . . shoulder.
10 The windscreen was smashed and the driver was cut in . . . face by
broken glass.
11 He was . . . very tall man with . . . dark hair and . . . small beard,
but I couldn't see . . . eyes because he was wearing . . . dark glasses.
12 He tore . . . trousers getting over a barbed wire fence.
13 Brother and sister were quite unlike each other. He had . . . fair
wavy hair; . . . hair was dark and straight.
14 She pulled . . . sleeve to attract his attention.
15 She pulled him by . . . sleeve.
16 'Hands up!' said the masked man, and we all put . . . hands up.
17 Ask . . . woman in front of you to take off . . . hat.
18 He stroked . . . chin thoughtfully.
19 If you're too hot why don't you take off . . . coat?
20 I saw him raise . . . right hand and take . . . oath.
21 The lioness bit him in . . . leg.
22 You should change . . . wet shoes, or you'll catch another cold.
23 There was a shot and a policeman came out with . . . blood running
down . . . face.
24 We shook . . . hands with . . . host.
25 He fell off his horse and injured . . . back.
26 The barman seized the drunk by . . . collar.
27 Leave . . . coats in . . . cloakroom; don't bring them into . . . theatre.
28 He fell down a flight of stairs and broke . . . rib.
29 He pointed to a woman in . . . green dress.
30 He is . . . thoroughly selfish man; he wouldn't lift . . . finger to help
anyone.
31 You'll strain . . . eyes if you read in . . . bad light.

32 She was on . . . knees, scrubbing . . . kitchen floor.
33 He has . . . horrible job; I wouldn't like to be in . . . shoes.
34 You've got . . . shirt on inside out.
35 'Pull up . . . socks,' said his mother.
36 I hit . . . thumb with a hammer when I was hanging the picture.

5 a/an and one

◪ PEG 4

Insert **a/an** or **one** if necessary.

1 . . . of my friends advised me to take . . . taxi; another said that
   there was quite . . . good bus service.
2 . . . friend of mine lent me . . . book by Meredith. I've only . . . more
   chapter to read. Would you like . . . loan of it afterwards? ~
   No, thanks. I read . . . of his books . . . few years ago and didn't like
   it. Besides I have . . . library book to finish. If I don't take it back
   tomorrow I'll have to pay . . . fine.
3 . . . man I met on the train told me . . . rather unusual story.
4 Most people like . . . rest after . . . hard day's work, but Tom
   seemed to have . . . inexhaustible supply of energy.
5 I've told you . . . hundred times not to come into . . . room with . . .
   hat on.
6 It's unlucky to light three cigarettes with . . . match. ~
   That's only . . . superstition. Only . . . idiot believes in superstitions.
7 He says . . . caravan is no good; he needs . . . cottage.
8 . . . plate is no good; we need . . . dozen.
9 Last time there was . . . fog here . . . plane crash-landed in . . . field
   near the airport. The crew had . . . lucky escape. . . . man broke his
   leg; the rest were unhurt.
10 You've been . . . great help to me; . . . day I will repay you.
11 My car broke down near . . . bus stop. There was . . . man waiting
   for . . . bus so I asked him for . . . advice.
12 He took . . . quick look at my car and said, 'Buy . . . new . . . .'
13 There was . . . woman there. The rest were men. ~
   There shouldn't have been even . . . woman. It was meant to be . . .
   stag party.
14 Don't tell . . . soul! Not even your wife! ~
   Of course not! I'd never tell . . . secret to . . . woman.
15 Most of the staff had been there for only . . . very short time, but
   . . . man had been there . . . year and . . . half, so he knew . . . little
   more than the rest.
16 Could you lend me . . . dictionary, please? I'm trying to do . . .
   crossword puzzle. ~
   I'm afraid I've only got . . . dictionary, and Tom's borrowed it.

17 ... chop won't be enough for Tom; he'll want two; he's ... small man but he's got ... big appetite.

18 'I want ... volunteers for ... dangerous job,' said the captain. There was ... long silence.
'Isn't there even ... man who will take ... risk?' he asked.
... voice called out from the back, 'Will there be ... reward?'

19 I have ... flat on the top floor. You get ... lovely view from there.

20 ... day a new director arrived. He was ... ambitious, bad-tempered man, and the staff took ... instant dislike to him.

21 Suddenly ... bullet struck ... street lamp ... little to Bill's left. He looked up and saw ... man with ... gun standing at ... open window.

22 Bill fired back twice. ... bullet hit the wall, the other broke ... pane of ... glass. He heard ... angry shout.

23 ... day—it was ... dry day with ... good visibility—Tom was driving along ... country road in ... borrowed car.

24 You're making ... mistake after another. Have you ... hangover, or something? ~
No, but I had ... very bad night last night. The people next door were having ... party. ~
... bad night shouldn't have such ... effect on your work. I often have three bad nights in succession. I live in ... very noisy street.

2 Auxiliary verbs

6 Auxiliary verbs

☐ PEG 106-7

Auxiliaries here are used both alone and as part of various tenses of ordinary verbs.

Read the following (a) in the negative (b) in the interrogative. These sentences, except for nos. 1 and 13, could also be used for question tag exercises (see Exercise 13).

Note:

1 **may** for possibility rarely begins a sentence. Instead we use **do you think (that)** + present/future or **is** + subject + **likely** + infinitive:

> Tom may know.
> Do you think (that) Tom knows?
> Is Tom likely to know?

2 Use **needn't** as the negative of **must**.

1 It may cost £100.
2 Men should help with the housework.
3 Tom would pay her.
4 They could play the guitar.
5 We're seeing Mary tomorrow.
6 She ought to keep it in the fridge.
7 You can understand it.
8 The police were watching the house.
9 You can go with him.
10 They've got a house.
11 Your boss will be angry.
12 Tom should pay the fine.
13 They may come tonight.
14 They were cleaning their shoes.
15 He must write in French.
16 You have read the instructions.
17 These pearls are made by oysters.
18 The ice was thick enough to walk on.
19 This will take a long time.
20 They may (*permission*) take the car.
21 You've made a mistake.
22 Ann would like a skiing holiday.

23 We must do it at once.
24 Tom could come.
25 They were in a hurry.
26 There is enough salt in it.
27 You could see the sea from the house.
28 Ann will be able to drive you.
29 They had written to him.
30 We must cook it in butter.
31 It is freezing.
32 She ought to accept the offer.
33 There'll be time for tea.
34 I'm right.
35 He may be at home.
36 He used to live here.

7 Auxiliaries conjugated with do/does/did

□ PEG 106–7, 123, 126 (see also Exercise 17)

Some auxiliaries when used in certain ways make their negative and interrogative according to the rule for ordinary verbs, i.e. with **do**. Sometimes either form is possible.

Make the sentences (a) negative and (b) interrogative, using **do/does/did**.

1 They have eggs for breakfast.
2 He needs a new coat.
3 He used to sell fruit.
4 They have to work hard.
5 She does the housework.
6 He needs more money.
7 He had a row with his boss.
8 She had a heart attack.
9 Her hair needed cutting.
10 He does his homework after supper.
11 She has a singing lesson every week.
12 She had to make a speech.
13 He does his best.
14 He has to get up at six every day.
15 The children have dinner at school.
16 She dared him to climb it.
17 You did it on purpose.
18 He has his piano tuned regularly. (*see 119*)
19 He dares to say that!
20 They had a good time.
21 The drink did him good.

22 My watch needs cleaning.
23 He had an accident.
24 You had your house painted.
25 She used to make her own clothes.
26 You do the exercises.
27 He had difficulty (in) getting a job.
28 He dared to interrupt the president, did he? (*Omit final* did he?)

8 Auxiliary verbs

☐ PEG 106-7

Put the following verbs into the past tense. (Auxiliaries are used both by themselves and as part of certain forms and tenses of ordinary verbs.)
Use **had to** as the past tense of **must** and **didn't need** as a past tense of **needn't**.

1 He isn't working hard.
2 She doesn't like cats.
3 I can't say anything.
4 We must read it carefully.
5 He won't help us.
6 He can lift it easily.
7 It isn't far from London.
8 Isn't it too heavy to carry?
9 He needn't pay at once.
10 He hopes that Tom will be there. (He hoped . . .)
11 How much does this cost?
12 He says that Ann may be there. (He said . . .)
13 How old is he?
14 Do you see any difference?
15 I do what I can.
16 How far can you swim?
17 I must change my shoes.
18 Tom dares not complain.
19 I don't dare (to) touch it.
20 Have you time to do it?
21 Are you frightened?
22 Must you pay for it yourself?
23 The letter needn't be typed.
24 We hope that he'll come. (We hoped. . .)
25 He says that she may not be in time. (He said that she . . .)
26 Do you understand what he is saying? I don't.
27 There are accidents every day at these crossroads.
28 She thinks that it may cost £100. (She thought that it . . .)
29 Doesn't Mr Pitt know your address?

30 They aren't expecting me, are they?
31 He thinks that the snakes may be dangerous. (*see 28*)
32 She wants to know if she can borrow the car. (She wanted to know if . . .)
33 Can't you manage on £100 a week?
34 Tom is certain that he will win.
35 Can you read the notice? No, I can't.
36 I don't think that the bull will attack us.

9 Auxiliary verbs

☐ PEG 108

Answer the following questions (a) in the affirmative (b) in the negative, in each case repeating the auxiliary and using a pronoun as subject.

Do you need this? ~ *Yes, I do/No, I don't.*
Can Tom swim? ~ *Yes, he can/No, he can't.*

Note also:

Is that Bill? ~ *Yes, it is/No, it isn't.*
Will there be time? ~ *Yes, there will/No, there won't.*

Use **needn't** in 7 and 15. Use **must** in 26 and 35.

1 Is the water deep?
2 Do you know the way?
3 Can you swim?
4 Does he come every day?
5 Is that Tom over there?
6 Are you Tom's brother?
7 Must you go?
8 Are you enjoying yourselves?
9 Did he see you?
10 Would £10 be enough?
11 May I borrow your car?
12 Is this the front of the queue?
13 Will she be there?
14 Do you play cards?
15 Should I tell the police?
16 Can you cook?
17 Are you ready?
18 Could women join the club?
19 Is your name Pitt?
20 Were they frightened?
21 Will his mother be there?
22 Ought I to get a new one?
23 Should I tell him the truth?

24 Was the driver killed?
25 Have you any money?
26 Need we finish the exercise?
27 Used he to ride in races?
28 Would you like to see him?
29 Is this yours?
30 Do you want it?
31 Can I take it?
32 Will you bring it back tomorrow?
33 Are you free this evening?
34 Am I in your way?
35 Need I wear a tie?
36 Was that Bill on the phone?

10 Additions to remarks, using auxiliary verbs

☐ PEG 112

Part 1 Add to the following remarks using **(and) so** + the
noun/pronoun in brackets + the auxiliary. If there is an auxiliary in
the first remark repeat this; if not use **do/does/did**.
   He lives in London. (I)   He lives in London *and so do I.*
   He had to wait. (you)   He had to wait *and so had you.*

1 I have read it. (John)
2 He is a writer. (she)
3 Tom can speak Welsh. (his wife)
4 She ought to get up. (you)
5 I should be wearing a seat belt. (you)
6 John will be there. (Tom)
7 The first bus was full. (the second)
8 I bought a ticket. (my brother)
9 You must come. (your son)
10 This bus goes to Piccadilly. (that)
11 I'm getting out at the next stop. (my friend)
12 He used to work in a restaurant. (I)

Part 2 Add to the following remarks using **(and) neither/nor** + the
auxiliary + the noun/pronoun in brackets.
   He isn't back. (she)   He isn't back *and neither is she.*

13 I haven't seen it. (Tom)
14 You shouldn't be watching TV. (Tom)
15 You mustn't be late. (I)
16 He can't come. (his sister)
17 I don't believe it. (Ann)
18 Alice couldn't understand. (Andrew)

19 I'm not going. (you)
20 This telephone doesn't work. (that)
21 Tom's car won't start. (mine)
22 I hadn't any change. (the taxi driver)
23 He didn't know the way. (anyone else)
24 My father wouldn't mind. (my mother)

Part 3 Contrary additions.
Add to the following remarks using **but** + noun/pronoun + the
auxiliary or **do/does/did**. Make a negative addition to an affirmative
remark:
    She thanked me. (he) She thanked me *but he didn't.*
Make an affirmative addition to a negative remark:
    She can't eat oysters. (I) She can't eat oysters *but I can.*

Use **needn't** as the negative of **must**, and **must** as the affirmative of
needn't.

25 John was seasick. (Mary)
26 He wasn't there. (she)
27 You must go. (your brother)
28 My sister can speak German. (I)
29 Alexander didn't want to wait. (James)
30 Bill needn't stay. (Stanley)
31 A cat wouldn't eat it. (a dog)
32 He will enjoy it. (his wife)
33 I haven't got a computer. (my neighbour)
34 This beach is safe for bathing. (that beach)
35 I must leave early. (you)
36 You don't have to pay tax. (I)

11 Agreements and disagreements with remarks, using auxiliary verbs

☐ PEG 109

Part 1 Agreements with affirmative remarks.
Agree with the following remarks, using **yes/so** + pronoun + the
auxiliary or **do/does/did**. To express surprise, use **Oh, so . . .**
    He has a good influence on her. ~ *Yes, he has.*

1 We must have a large room.
2 I was very rude.
3 She always wears dark glasses.
4 She may be a spy.
5 Tom could tell us where to go.
6 There's a snake in that basket.

Auxiliary verbs

7 He needs six bottles.
8 This boat is leaking!
9 His revolver was loaded.
10 This restaurant might be expensive.
11 They used to have a parrot.
12 The fog is getting thicker.

Part 2 Agreements with negative remarks.
Agree with the following remarks, using **no** + pronoun + the auxiliary.
   Elephants never forget. ~ *No, they don't.*

13 Cuckoos don't build nests.
14 He didn't complain.
15 It isn't worth keeping.
16 He can't help coughing.
17 The ice wasn't thick enough.
18 The lift wouldn't come down.
19 This flat hasn't got very thick walls.
20 They don't have earthquakes there.
21 The oranges didn't look very good.
22 It hasn't been a bad summer.
23 I don't look my age.
24 He mightn't like that colour.

Part 3 Disagreements with affirmative or negative remarks.
Disagree with the following remarks, using **oh no/but** + pronoun + auxiliary. Use a negative auxiliary if the first verb is affirmative and an affirmative auxiliary if the first verb is negative.
   He won't be any use. ~ *(Oh) yes, he will.*
   She worked here for a year. ~ *(Oh) no, she didn't.*

25 You're drunk.
26 I didn't do it on purpose.
27 They weren't in your way.
28 I wasn't born then.
29 She'd rather live alone.
30 You gave him my address.
31 I can use your bicycle.
32 That five pound note belongs to me.
33 He didn't mean to be rude.
34 Children get too much pocket money.
35 Exams should be abolished.
36 She promised to obey him.

12 Question tags after negative statements

☐ PEG 110

Add question tags to the following statements.
Bill doesn't know Ann.
Bill doesn't know Ann, does he?
Ann hasn't got a phone.
Ann hasn't got a phone, has she?

this/that (subject) becomes **it** in the tag. **there** remains unchanged:
That isn't Tom, is it?
There won't be time, will there?

All the tags, except the tag for no. 30, should be spoken in the usual way with a statement intonation. But they could also be practised with a question intonation. The important word in the statement must then be stressed.

1 You aren't afraid of snakes.
2 Ann isn't at home.
3 You don't know French.
4 Tom didn't see her.
5 This isn't yours.
6 Mary wasn't angry.
7 Bill hasn't had breakfast.
8 You won't tell anyone.
9 I didn't wake you up.
10 Tom doesn't like oysters.
11 You don't want to sell the house.
12 It doesn't hurt.
13 People shouldn't drink and drive.
14 You aren't going alone.
15 They couldn't pay the rent.
16 You don't agree with Bill.
17 There wasn't a lot to do.
18 I needn't say anything.
19 That wasn't Ann on the phone.
20 You didn't do it on purpose.
21 This won't take long.
22 She doesn't believe you.
23 It didn't matter very much.
24 He shouldn't put so much salt in it.
25 Mary couldn't leave the children alone.
26 You aren't doing anything tonight.
27 You wouldn't mind helping me with this.
28 George hadn't been there before.
29 The children weren't surprised.
30 You wouldn't like another drink.

31 Tom doesn't have to go to lectures.
32 Bill hasn't got a car.
33 Bill couldn't have prevented it.
34 I needn't wait any longer.
35 There weren't any mosquitoes.
36 The fire wasn't started deliberately.

13 Question tags after affirmative statements

◢ PEG 110

Add question tags to the following statements:
    Tom goes to Bath quite often, *doesn't he?*
    He told you about his last trip, *didn't he?*
    It was very cold last night, *wasn't it?*

Be careful of the contractions **'s** and **'d**:
    He's ready, *isn't he?*   He's finished, *hasn't he?*
    He'd seen it, *hadn't he?* He'd like it, *wouldn't he?*

These should be practised mainly with a statement intonation, but they could also be said with a question intonation. See notes to previous exercise.

1 The children can read French.
2 He's ten years old.
3 Bill came on a bicycle.
4 The Smiths have got two cars.
5 Your grandfather was a millionaire.
6 Tom should try again.
7 It could be done.
8 Your brother's here.
9 That's him over there.
10 George can leave his case here.
11 This will fit in your pocket.
12 His wife has headaches quite often.
13 She's got lovely blue eyes.
14 The twins arrived last night.
15 Mary paints portraits.
16 Bill puts the money in the bank.
17 Bill put the money in the bank.
18 Prices keep going up.
19 I've seen you before.
20 Bill's written a novel.
21 His mother's very proud of him.
22 The twins used to play rugby.
23 Tom might be at home now.
24 We must hurry.

25 You'd been there before.
26 You'd like a drink.
27 The boys prefer a cooked breakfast.
28 Mary ought to cook it for them.
29 That was Ann on the phone.
30 The Smiths need two cars.
31 You'll help me.
32 He used to eat raw fish.
33 There'll be plenty for everyone.
34 You'd better wait for Bill.
35 You'd come if I needed help.
36 You could come at short notice.

14 Question tags: mixed

☑ PEG 110

See notes to Exercises 12 and 13.
Note that a statement containing words such as **none, nobody,
hardly/hardly any** etc. is treated as a negative statement:
    He hardly ever makes a mistake, does he?

When the subject is **nobody/anybody/everybody** etc., the pronoun
they is used in the tag:
    Nobody liked the play, did they?

Add question tags to the following statements.

1 You take sugar in tea.
2 But you don't take it in coffee.
3 The lift isn't working today.
4 It never works very well.
5 The area was evacuated at once.
6 There was no panic.
7 Though everybody realized the danger.
8 There was a lot of noise.
9 But nobody complained.
10 Mary hardly ever cooks.
11 She buys convenience foods.
12 She'd save money if she bought fresh food.
13 Mr Smith usually remembered his wife's birthdays.
14 But he didn't remember this one.
15 And his wife was very disappointed.
16 He ought to have made a note of it.
17 Neither of them offered to help you.
18 They don't allow pet dogs in this shop.
19 But guide dogs can come in.
20 He hardly ever leaves the house.

21 That isn't Bill driving.
22 Nothing went wrong.
23 Lions are loose in this reserve.
24 So we'd better get back in the car.
25 It'd be unpleasant to be attacked by a lion.
26 And it wouldn't be any use running away.
27 It is a pity Ann didn't come with us.
28 She'd have enjoyed it.
29 They should have planned the expedition more carefully.
30 Lives were lost unnecessarily.
31 She warned him not to ride the stallion.
32 But he never takes advice.
33 There used to be trees here.
34 There isn't any point in waiting.
35 He'll hardly come now.
36 Your central heating doesn't work very well.

15 Auxiliaries followed by full or bare infinitive

☐ PEG 246

Put **to** where necessary before the infinitives in brackets.

1 You needn't (come) tomorrow.
2 People used (travel) on horseback.
3 I'll have (hurry).
4 You ought (take) a holiday.
5 I'll (lend) him some money.
6 You are (go) at once.
7 We didn't have (pay) anything.
8 There won't (be) enough room for everyone.
9 You can (see) the windmill from here.
10 He was able (explain).
11 We may have (stay) here all night.
12 He used (spend) a lot of time in his library.
13 He didn't dare (say) anything.
14 Don't (move).
15 We'll (look) for a hotel.
16 You needn't (look) for a hotel; I'll be able (put) you up.
17 The doctor said that I ought (give up) smoking.
18 He used (drink) quite a lot.
19 He should (be) ready by now.
20 May I (ask) you a question?
21 I shan't be able (do) it till after the holidays.
22 I didn't need (say) anything.
23 How dare you (open) my letters!
24 They ought (warn) people about the dangerous currents.

25 I should (say) nothing about it if I were you.
26 You are not (mention) this to anyone.
27 Why do they (obey) him? ~
   They don't dare (refuse).
28 You must (look) both ways before crossing the road.
29 Your map may (have been) out of date.
30 You ought (have finished) it last night.
31 I must (say) I think you behaved very badly.
32 I will have (carry) a tent.
33 We've got (get out).
34 It might (kill) somebody.
35 Ought you (be) watching TV?
36 Shouldn't you (be) doing your homework?

16 Auxiliaries: mixed

◪ PEG chapters 11–16

Fill each of the following gaps with a suitable auxiliary or auxiliary
form.

1 Schoolboy to friend: I left my book at home. . . . I share yours?
2 I'm taking swimming lessons. I hope to . . . to swim by the end of
  the month.
3 You . . . better take off your wet shoes.
4 I'm sorry I'm late. I . . . to wait ages for a bus.
5 Teacher: You . . . (*obligation*) read the play, but you . . . (*no
  obligation*) read the preface.
6 I knew he was wrong but I . . . (*hadn't the courage*) to tell him so.
7 You're getting fat. You . . . to cut down on your beer drinking.
8 He . . . to smoke very heavily. Now he hardly smokes at all.
9 The new motorway . . . opened this afternoon. (*plan*)
10 I've come without any money. . . . you possibly lend me £5?
11 Ann: . . . we meet at Piccadilly Circus?
12 Tom: It . . . be better to meet at the theatre. We . . . miss one
   another at Piccadilly.
13 . . . you like to come canoeing with me next weekend?
14 Mary: I . . . to pay 20p. for this little chap on the bus yesterday.
15 Ann: My little boy's under three so I . . . (*No obligation. Use present
   tense.*) to pay for him.
16 The plane . . . landed (*unfulfilled plan*) at Heathrow, but it has been
   diverted to Gatwick.
17 You've spelt it wrong. There . . . be another 's'.
18 You . . . told me! (*I'm disappointed that you didn't tell me.*)
19 We . . . to take a taxi. Otherwise we'll be late.

20 At the holiday camp we . . . to get up at six and bathe in the river. Then we . . . come back and cook an enormous breakfast. (*routine actions*)
21 Tom . . . know the address. (*Tom probably knows.*)
22 Tom . . . know the address. (*I'm sure that Tom knows.*)
23 I've lost my umbrella! I . . . left it on the bus! (*deduction*)
24 Theatre regulations: At the end of the performance the public . . . (*are permitted to*) leave by all exit doors.
25 If I . . . you I'd get a taxi.
26 Did you paint it yourself or did you . . . it painted?
27 You . . . (*negative*) to be driving so fast. There's a speed limit here.
28 You . . . (*request*) get me some aspirin when you're at the chemist's.

17 have: possessive

◢ PEG 122

In British English, **have** meaning **possess** is not normally conjugated with **do** except when there is an idea of habit.

> *I haven't* (*got*) a watch.　　(present possession)
> How many corners *has* a　　(a characteristic rather than a habit)
> cube?
> He *doesn't* usually *have* time　(habit)
> to study.

In the past, **did** is used for habit; otherwise either form is possible:
> *Did you have/Had you* an umbrella when you left the house?

In other English-speaking countries, however, the **do** forms are used almost exclusively. It would therefore be possible to use **do/did** forms throughout the following exercises (except in no. 27), but students are asked to use **have not/have you** forms where they could be used. Where both are equally usual this will be noted in the key.

Fill the spaces with the correct forms of **have**, adding **got** where possible. Only one space will be left in each clause, but note that **got** may be separated from **have** by another word. When a negative form is required '(*negative*)' will be placed at the end of the example.

1 He is standing there in the rain and . . . even the sense to put up his umbrella. (*negative*)
2 He . . . a cold in the head. ~
  That's nothing new; he always . . . a cold.
3 I . . . brainwaves very often, but I . . . one now. (*1st verb negative*)
4 It is no good arguing with someone who . . . a bee in his bonnet.
5 Why don't you say something? You . . . an excuse? (*negative*)
6 You . . . this toothache yesterday?
7 How many letters . . . the alphabet?

8 The houses in your country . . . flat roofs?
9 You . . . the time? (= Do you know the time?) ~
   No, I . . . a watch. (*negative*)
10 You ever . . . an impulse to smash something?
11 He . . . £1,000 a year when his father dies.
12 Air passengers usually . . . much luggage. (*negative*)
13 You . . . any objection to sitting with your back to the engine?
14 Oysters . . . always pearls in them. (*negative*)
15 Your door . . . a little hole through which you can peep at callers?
   (*negative*)
16 You . . . a match on you? ~
   No, I don't smoke so I never . . . matches.
17 What is your opinion? ~
   I . . . an opinion. (*negative*)
18 That cup . . . a crack in it.
19 You . . . any suspicion who did it?
20 This desk . . . a secret drawer? ~
   No, modern desks ever . . . secret drawers. (*negative*)
21 When you go to a place for the first time, you ever . . . a feeling that
   you've been there before?
22 Babies . . . teeth when they're born?
23 How many sides . . . a pentagon?
24 Our cat . . . kittens every year. ~
   How many she . . . each time?
25 They say that if children . . . complete freedom when they are
   young, they . . . inhibitions when they grow up. (*2nd verb negative*)
26 You . . . mosquitoes in your country in summer?
27 You . . . children? ~
   Yes, I . . . two, a boy and a girl.
28 You . . . a motor cycle? ~
   No, I only . . . an ordinary bicycle, but I . . . a motor cycle next year.
29 Why do you suddenly want to back out? You . . . cold feet?
30 Customer: You . . . any mushrooms today?
   Shopkeeper: We usually . . . them but I'm afraid we . . . any at the
   moment. (*last verb negative*)
31 I think I know the man you mean. He . . . one blue eye and one
   brown one? (*negative*)
32 Children nowadays . . . far too much pocket money. I . . . any when I
   was at school. (*2nd verb negative*)
33 We were always getting lost in the desert. ~
   You . . . compasses? (*negative*)
34 Red-haired people always . . . bad tempers?
35 Do you think we should eat this meat? It . . . a very nice smell.
   (*negative*)
36 The stairs are on fire! You . . . a long rope?

18 have: various uses

■ PEG 123

have can mean take (a meal/lesson/bath, etc.), entertain (guests), encounter (difficulty, etc.), enjoy (a time/journey, etc.). When used in these ways:
(a) have usually forms its negative and interrogative with do.
(b) have can be used in the continuous tenses.

Put the correct form of have into the following sentences. Use am having, is having, etc., as a future form.

1 We . . . some friends in for dinner tomorrow night.
2 You . . . a good journey yesterday?
3 Don't disturb him; he . . . a rest.
4 We . . . lunch early tomorrow.
5 How many lessons he . . . a week? ~
   He usually . . . four.
6 You . . . earthquakes in your country?
7 What time you . . . breakfast? ~
   We usually . . . it at 8.00.
8 What you . . . for breakfast? ~
   We . . . toast and coffee.
9 Why you . . . a cooked breakfast? (negative) ~
   It's too much trouble.
10 Why were they making such a noise? ~
   They . . . an argument.
11 You . . . a thunderstorm yesterday?
12 Come in, we . . . a debate.
13 You . . . a cup of coffee? ~
   Yes, please.
14 We . . . a meeting tomorrow to discuss safety precautions.
15 The tree just missed the roof, we . . . a very lucky escape.
16 How did you damage your car? You . . . an accident?
17 I . . . a look at that house tomorrow. If I like it I'll buy it.
18 We . . . very bad weather just now.
19 I . . . a very interesting conversation with the milkman when my neighbour interrupted me.
20 English people always . . . roast beef for lunch on Sundays?
21 It is difficult to learn a foreign language when you . . . an opportunity of speaking it. (negative)
22 The farmers . . . a lot of trouble with foxes at present.
23 On the whole women drivers . . . so many accidents as men drivers. (negative)
24 You . . . anything to eat before you left home? ~
   Oh yes, I . . . bacon and eggs.
25 You . . . any difficulty getting into your flat last night?

26 Are you enjoying yourself? ~
   Yes, I . . . a wonderful time.
27 How often he . . . a singing lesson?
28 You . . . a good night? ~
   No, I slept very badly.
29 Why were they late? ~
   They . . . a puncture.
30 We . . . a party here next week. Would you like to come?
31 Why didn't you speak to her? ~
   I . . . a chance. (*negative*)
32 We . . . a lecture next Monday.
33 I . . . tea with her tomorrow.
34 He . . . an operation next week.
35 He ever . . . nightmares?
36 When he got tired of it I . . . a try. ~
   You . . . any luck? ~
   Yes, I caught a great big fish.

19 The **have** + object + past participle construction

☑ PEG 119

Part 1 Fill in the spaces by inserting the correct form of **have**. Use **am/is/are having** as a future form. (**get** can be used instead of **have**, but is more colloquial.)

1 I . . . my house painted. That is why there is all this mess.
2 My hair looks dreadful; I think I . . . it set tomorrow.
3 The attic was dark so last year we . . . skylight put in.
4 That dead tree is dangerous. I . . . it cut down tomorrow.
5 We . . . just . . . central heating installed. The house is warm!
6 I can't read Greek so I . . . the documents translated. My nephew is helping with the translation.
7 . . . you . . . the film developed or did you develop it yourself?
8 Why . . . he . . . all his shoes specially made?
   He says that he has to because his feet are different sizes.
9 . . . you . . . your milk delivered or do you go to the shop for it?
10 If you hate cleaning fish why . . . you . . . them cleaned at the fishmonger's? (*negative*)
11 How often . . . you . . . your brakes tested?
12 I'm afraid it's rather draughty here but I . . . that broken pane replaced tomorrow.

Part 2 Fill in the spaces by inserting the correct form of **have**, the past participle of the verb in brackets and, where necessary, a pronoun.

13 Your ankle is very swollen. You'd better . . . it . . . (x-ray)
14 Your roof is leaking, you should . . . it . . . (repair)
15 The trousers are too long; I must . . . (shorten)
16 No one will be able to read your notes. ~
   I know; I . . . them . . . (type)
17 That's a good piano but you should . . . it . . . (tune)
18 Why don't you . . . the document . . . ? (photocopy)
19 He didn't like the colour of the curtains so he . . . (dye)
20 He went to a garage to . . . the puncture . . . (mend)
21 His arm was broken so he had to go to hospital to . . . (set)
22 The battery is all right now. I . . . just . . . it . . . (recharge)
23 It's a beautiful photo. I'm going to . . . (enlarge)
24 Be careful of those knives. I . . . just . . . (sharpen)

Part 3 Rewrite the sentences using a **have** + object + past participle construction and omitting the words in bold type.
   I **employed a plumber** to examine my boiler.
   I had my boiler examined.

25 I **pay a garage** to service my car.
26 The tap keeps dripping so I must **send for a plumber** to see to it.
27 I **paid a watchmaker** to clean my watch.
28 **An artist** is painting her portrait. She . . .
29 They **arranged for the police** to arrest the man.
30 He **paid a lorry** driver to tow the car to a garage.
31 They are **employing builders** to build a garage.
32 I **pay a window cleaner** to clean my windows every month.
33 I **went to an oculist and** he tested my eyes for me.
34 **The old gypsy** is telling Tom's fortune. Tom . . .
35 I **asked the fishmonger** to open the oysters **for me**.
36 I **went to a jeweller and he** pierced my ears **for me**.

20 be

■ PEG 113–17, 290, 293, 300, 302

This is a general exercise which includes infinitives, subjunctives, conditionals, and some examples of the **be** + infinitive construction. When this last construction or a passive construction is required the second verb is given in brackets at the end of the sentence.
   Why are all those dogs wearing harness? ~
   They . . . as guide dogs for the blind. (train)
   They are being trained as guide dogs for the blind.

Fill the spaces in the following sentences by inserting the correct form of **be** with, where necessary, the past participle or present or perfect infinitive of the verb in brackets.

Remember that, in the passive, **be** can be used in the continuous tenses.

1 They are cutting down all the trees. The countryside . . . (ruin)
2 The Prime Minister . . . a speech tonight. (make)
3 If I . . . you I'd go on to the next exercise.
4 . . . late once is excusable but . . . late every day is not.
5 He ordered that all lights . . . (extinguish)
6 How long you . . . here?
7 My flat was full of dust because the old house just opposite . . . (pull down)
8 He asked where he . . . it. (put)
   I told him to put it on the mantelpiece.
9 It . . . difficult to read a newspaper upside down? (*Use negative.*)
10 You . . . here till I return. That is an order. (stay)
11 He suggests that prominent people . . . to contribute. (ask)
12 Even if you . . . to go on your knees to him I don't think it would make him change his mind.
13 I . . . on a catering course when I leave school. My parents have arranged it. (go)
14 What is happening now? ~
   The injured man . . . out of the arena. (carry)
15 It's better . . . too early than too late.
16 I wish you . . . here. I miss you very much.
17 Why did you leave him behind? You . . . him with you. (*Those were your instructions.*) (take)
18 She is learning Italian. She . . . by a professor from Milan. (teach)
19 I know I . . . half an hour late yesterday but I . . . half an hour early tomorrow. ~
   I'd rather you . . . punctual every day. (*see 297*)
20 It is impossible . . . right every time.
21 He . . . here by seven but now it's nine and there's no sign of him. (be)
22 They decided that voting papers . . . to all members. (send)
23 There . . . eggs for breakfast tomorrow?
24 If only I . . . there! (But I wasn't.)
25 The Queen . . . the new hospital next week. (open)
26 I couldn't see the man who was guiding us and I didn't know where we . . . (take)
27 It . . . a trilogy but in the end the author found that he had only enough material for two volumes. (be)
28 You . . . very angry if I refused?
29 The matter . . . discussed in tomorrow's debate.

30 His mare ... in tomorrow's race but he said this morning that she was sick and wouldn't be running after all. (run)
31 The house wasn't ready; it still ... and there were pots of paint and ladders everywhere. (paint)
32 They decided that an expurgated edition ... for use in schools. (print)
33 His works are immensely popular; they ... into all the major European languages. (translate)
34 It is high time you ... in bed.
35 I had my instructions and I knew exactly what I ... (do)
36 If this report ... believed, we are going to have a very severe drought.

21 it is/there is

■ PEG 67, 116–17

Insert **it is/there is** in the spaces. In some sentences, contracted plural, negative and interrogative forms, or the past or future tense are required.

1 What's the time? ~ ... ... 3.30. ~
And what's the date? ~ ... ... the 24th.
2 How far ... ... to York? ~
... ... 50 miles.
3 ... ... very stormy last night. ~
Yes, ... storms all over the country.
4 ... ... freezing very hard. ... ... ice on the lake tomorrow.
5 As ... ... sunny she decided to take the children to the sea.
6 Why don't you go for a walk? ... ... a pity to stay in when ... ... so nice outside.
7 ... ... not any shadows because ... ... not any sun.
8 ... ... going to be a bus strike tomorrow. ~
... ... all right if ... ... a fine day; but if ... ... wet
... ... long queues on the Underground.
9 ... ... not any glass in the windows; that is why ... ... so cold in the room.
10 ... ... very wet yesterday; ... ... impossible to go out.
11 ... ... a lot of rain last week. ... ... floods everywhere.
12 ... ... a thick fog last night. ... ... several accidents on the motorway.
13 ... ... foolish to drive fast when ... ... foggy.
14 ... ... difficult to find your way round this town. ... ... so many streets all looking exactly alike.
15 Come on, children! ... ... time to get up! ... ... nearly breakfast time.

16 . . . . lunch time when we get to York, so let's have lunch there. ~
No, ... not be time for lunch because our train to Edinburgh leaves York at 13.15.
17 . . . . . . a funny smell here. . . . . . . turpentine?
18 . . . . . . all sorts of stories about Robin Hood, but . . . . . . not known exactly who he was or what he did.
19 . . . . . . said that if you break a mirror you'll be unlucky for seven years.
20 As he had very bad sight . . . . . . difficult for him to recognize people.
21 'Can I have a *Telegraph*, please?' said the customer.
'I'm afraid . . . . . . not any left,' said the newsagent. 'But . . . . . . a *Guardian* on the rack beside you. Why not take that? . . . . . . just as good.'
22 . . . . . . not necessary to carry your passport everywhere with you but . . . . . . advisable to carry some document of identity.
23 . . . . . . a guard outside the door and . . . . . . bars on the windows.
. . . . . . impossible to escape.
24 . . . . . . a garage behind the hotel? ~
Yes, but . . . . . . rather full. I don't think . . . . . . room for your car.
25 One night . . . . . . a heavy fall of snow which blocked all the roads. Luckily . . . . . . plenty of food in the house.
26 . . . . . . a hotel in the village, so we decided to stay there.
. . . . . . a charming village and I was very happy there, but my children were bored because . . . . . . nothing to do in the evenings.
27 . . . . . . five flats in the building—one on each floor. Mine's on the top floor. . . . . . . no lift but . . . . . . supposed to be good for the figure to run up and down stairs, ...?
28 . . . . . . a pity you haven't another bedroom. ~
Yes, but . . . . . . quite a big loft, which I am thinking of turning into a bedroom. . . . . . . a skylight so . . . . . . not . . . a ventilation problem.
29 . . . . . . all sorts of legends about these caves. . . . . . . said that smugglers hid their goods here and that . . . . . . an underground passage leading to the village inn.
30 Tell me something about *King Lear*. ~
. . . . . . the story of a king who divided his kingdom between his daughters. . . . . . . foolish to give away your property like that. . . .
. . . never certain that your family will behave generously to you in return.
31 Has Tom any more children? ~
Yes. . . . . . . a daughter, Ann. ~
Oh yes, ... Ann who opened the door to us yesterday, ...?
32 He thought that . . . . . . better to say nothing about his change of plan.

33 ... ... a long time before I got an answer. Then one day a letter arrived—well, ... not really a letter, for ... ... only one sentence on the paper.

34 ... ... a pond beside your house? ~ Yes, ... ~
How deep ... ...?

35 We've done all we can. ... ... nothing to do now but wait.

36 Just cross out that word and go on. ... ... not necessary to begin again. (or ... ... no need to begin again.)

22 can and be able

◪ PEG 136–8

Part 1 can, used to express ability with could, shall/will be able

Fill the following spaces, using **can** for present, **could** for past and **shall/will be able** for future. There is no need to use other **able** forms in this section. Put **to** where necessary before the infinitives.

1 ... you stand on your head? ~
I ... when I was at school but I ... now. (*2nd verb negative*)

2 When I've passed my driving test I ... hire a car from our local garage.

3 At the end of the month the Post Office will send him an enormous telephone bill which he ... pay. (*negative*)

4 I ... remember the address. (*negative*) ~
... you even remember the street? (*negative*)

5 When the fog lifts we ... see where we are.

6 You've put too much in your rucksack; you never ... carry all that.

7 When I was a child I ... understand adults, and now that I am an adult I ... understand children. (*negative, negative*)

8 When you have taken your degree you ... put letters after your name?

9 Don't try to look at all the pictures in the gallery. Otherwise when you get home you ... remember any of them. (*negative*)

10 When I first went to Spain I ... read Spanish but I ... speak it. (*2nd verb negative*)

11 ... you type? ~
Yes, I ... type but I ... do shorthand. (*2nd verb negative*)

12 I'm locked in. I ... get out! (*negative*) ~
... you squeeze between the bars? (*negative*) ~
No! I ...; I'm too fat. (*negative*)

Part 2   could and was able

In some of the following sentences either **could** or **was able** could be used. In others only **was/were able** is possible. Fill the spaces and put **to** where necessary before the infinitives.

13 He was very strong; he . . . ski all day and dance all night.
14 The car plunged into the river. The driver . . . get out but the passengers were drowned.
15 I was a long way from the stage. I . . . see all right but I . . . hear very well. (*2nd verb negative*)
16 We . . . borrow umbrellas; so we didn't get wet.
17 . . . you walk or did they have to carry you?
18 I had no key so I . . . lock the door. (*negative*)
19 I knew the town so I . . . advise him where to go.
20 When the garage had repaired our car we . . . continue our journey.
21 At five years old he . . . read quite well.
22 When I arrived everyone was asleep. Fortunately I . . . wake my sister and she let me in.
23 The swimmer was very tired but he . . . reach the shore before he collapsed.
24 The police were suspicious at first but I . . . convince them that we were innocent.

Part 3   PEG 222 C, 223 B, 283-4

This section includes examples of **could** used for polite requests and as a conditional.

25 . . . I speak to Mr Pitt, please? ~
I'm afraid he's out at the moment. . . . you ring back later?
26 If you stood on my shoulders . . . you reach the top of the wall? ~
No, I'm afraid I . . . (*negative*)
27 If I sang . . . you accompany me on the piano? ~
No, I . . ., I . . . play the piano! (*negative, negative*)
28 If a letter comes for me . . . you please forward it to this address?
29 She made the wall very high so that boys . . . climb over it. (*negative*)
30 They took his passport so that he . . . leave the country. (*negative*)
31 . . . you tell me the time, please? ~
I'm afraid I. . . . I haven't got a watch. (*negative*)
32 If you had to, . . . you go without food for a week? ~
I suppose I . . . if I had plenty of water.
33 . . . you lend me £5? ~
No, I . . . (*negative*)
34 They used to chain valuable books to library desks so that people . . . take them away. (*negative*)
35 He says that he saw Clementine drowning but . . . help her as he . . . swim. (*negative, negative*)
36 If you had had the right tools . . . you have repaired the engine?

23 may

☐ PEG 127–33, 285, 288, 340

Insert the correct form of **may/might** except in 10 and 36, where a
be allowed form is necessary.

1 It . . . rain, you'd better take a coat.
2 He said that it . . . rain.
3 We . . . as well stay here till the weather improves.
4 . . . I borrow your umbrella?
5 You . . . tell me! (*I think I have a right to know.*)
6 Candidates . . . not bring textbooks into the examination room.
7 People convicted of an offence . . . (*have a right to*) appeal.
8 If he knew our address he . . . come and see us.
9 . . . I come in? ~
   Please do.
10 When he was a child he . . . (*they let him*) do exactly as he liked.
11 I think I left my glasses in your office. You . . . ask your secretary to
   look for them for me. (*request*)
12 He . . . be my brother (*I admit that he is*) but I don't trust him.
13 I . . . never see you again.
14 He . . . be on the next train. We . . . as well wait.
15 If we got there early we . . . get a good seat.
16 The police . . . (*have a right to*) ask a driver to take a breath test.
17 You ought to buy now; prices . . . go up.
18 I'll wait a week so that he . . . have time to think it over.
19 He isn't going to eat it; I . . . as well give it to the dog.
20 You . . . at least read the letter. (*I think you should.*)
21 You . . . have written. (*I am annoyed/disappointed that you didn't.*)
22 We'd better be early; there . . . be a crowd.
23 Nobody knows how people first came to these islands. They . . .
   have sailed from South America on rafts.
24 You . . . (*have permission to*) use my office.
25 He said that we . . . use his office whenever we liked.
26 I don't think I'll succeed but I . . . as well try.
27 You ought to go to his lectures, you . . . learn something.
28 If we can give him a blood transfusion we . . . be able to save his
   life.
29 Two parallel white lines in the middle of the road mean that you . . .
   not overtake.
30 If I bought a lottery ticket I . . . win £1,000.
31 If you said that, he . . . be very offended.
32 I wonder why they didn't go. ~
   The weather . . . have been too bad.
33 Warning: No part of this book . . . be reproduced without the
   publisher's permission.
34 He has refused, but he . . . change his mind if you asked him again.

35 ... I see your passport, please?
36 He ... (*negative*) drive since his accident. (*They haven't let him drive.*)

24 **must** and **have to**

▰ PEG 144–5

Fill the spaces in the following sentences by inserting **must** or the present, future, or past form of **have to**.

1 She ... leave home at eight every morning at present.
2 Notice in a picture gallery: Cameras, sticks and umbrellas ... be left at the desk.
3 He sees very badly; he ... wear glasses all the time.
4 I ... do all the typing at my office.
5 You ... read this book. It's really excellent.
6 The children ... play in the streets till their mothers get home from work.
7 She felt ill and ... leave early.
8 Mr Pitt ... cook his own meals. His wife is away.
9 I hadn't enough money and I ... pay by cheque.
10 I never remember his address; I always ... look it up.
11 Employer: You ... come to work in time.
12 If you go to a dentist with a private practice you ... pay him quite a lot of money.
13 Father to small son: You ... do what Mummy says.
14 My neighbour's child ... practise the piano for three hours a day.
15 Doctor: I can't come now.
   Caller: You ... come; he's terribly ill.
16 English children ... stay at school till the age of 16.
17 In my district there is no gas laid on. People ... use electricity for everything.
18 Notice above petrol pump: All engines ... be switched off.
19 Mother to daughter: You ... come in earlier at night.
20 The shops here don't deliver. We ... carry everything home ourselves.
21 The buses were all full; I ... get a taxi.
22 Notice beside escalators: Dogs and push chairs ... be carried.
23 'Au pair' girls usually ... do quite a lot of housework.
24 Tell her that she ... be here by six. I insist on it.
25 When a tyre is punctured the driver ... change the wheel.
26 Park notice: All dogs ... be kept on leads.
27 She ... learn how to drive when her local railway station is closed.
28 Railway notice: Passengers ... cross the line by the footbridge.
29 I got lost and ... ask a policeman the way.
30 Farmers ... get up early.

31 If you buy that television set you . . . buy a licence for it.
32 When I changed my job I . . . move to another flat.
33 Waiters . . . pay tax on the tips that they receive.
34 Father to son: I can't support you any longer; you . . . earn your own living from now on.
35 Railway notice: Passengers . . . be in possession of a ticket.
36 Whenever the dog wants to go out I . . . get up and open the door.

25 **must not** and **need not**

☐ PEG 146

Use **must not** or **need not** to fill the spaces in the following sentences.

1 You . . . ring the bell; I have a key.
2 Notice in cinema: Exit doors . . . be locked during performances.
3 You . . . drink this: it is poison.
4 We . . . drive fast; we have plenty of time.
5 You . . . drive fast; there is a speed limit here.
6 Candidates . . . bring books into the examination room.
7 You . . . write to him for he will be here tomorrow.
8 We . . . make any noise or we'll wake the baby.
9 You . . . bring an umbrella. It isn't going to rain.
10 You . . . do all the exercise. Ten sentences will be enough.
11 We . . . reheat the pie. We can eat it cold.
12 Mother to child: You . . . tell lies.
13 You . . . turn on the light; I can see quite well.
14 You . . . strike a match; the room is full of gas.
15 You . . . talk to other candidates during the exam.
16 We . . . make any more sandwiches; we have plenty now.
17 You . . . put salt in any of his dishes. Salt is very bad for him.
18 You . . . take anything out of a shop without paying for it.
19 You . . . carry that parcel home yourself; the shop will send it.
20 You . . . clean the windows. The window-cleaner is coming tomorrow.
21 Mother to child: You . . . play with matches.
22 Church notice: Visitors . . . walk about the church during a service.
23 I . . . go to the shops today. There is plenty of food in the house.
24 You . . . smoke in a non-smoking compartment.
25 Police notice: Cars . . . be parked here.
26 We . . . open the lion's cage. It is contrary to Zoo regulations.
27 You . . . make your bed. The maid will do it.
28 I want this letter typed but you . . . do it today. Tomorrow will do.

29 I'll lend you the money and you . . . pay me back till next month.
30 We . . . climb any higher; we can see very well from here.
31 You . . . look under the bed. There isn't anybody there.
32 You . . . ask a woman her age. It's not polite.
33 You've given me too much. ~
   You . . . eat it all.
34 We . . . forget to shut the lift gates.
35 Mother to child: You . . . interrupt when I am speaking.
36 If you want the time, pick up the receiver and dial 8081; you . . . say
   anything.

26 need not and don't have to etc.

■ PEG 148–50

Replace the words in bold type by **need not/need I?** etc., or a
negative or interrogative **have to** form.
> I've been invited to a wedding; but I can't go. **Will it be
> necessary for me** to send a present?
> *Shall I have to send a present?*

1 **It isn't necessary for him to** go on working. He has already reached
   retiring age. (*He . . .*)
2 **Was it necessary for you to** wait a long time for your bus?
3 **It isn't necessary for me to** water my tomato plants every day.
4 **It will be necessary for them to** get up early when they go out to
   work every day.
5 We had to stop at the frontier but we **were not required to** open our
   cases.
6 **It wasn't necessary to** walk. He took us in his car. (*We . . .*)
7 My employer said, '**I shan't require** you tomorrow.' (*You . . . come.*)
8 **It is never necessary for me to** work on Saturdays.
9 When I am eighteen I'll be of age. Then **it won't be necessary to** live
   at home if I don't want to.
10 New teacher to his class: **It isn't necessary for you to** call me 'Sir';
   call me 'Bill'.
11 **Will it be necessary for us to** report this accident to the police?
12 When you buy something on the instalment system you **are not
   required to** pay the whole price at once.
13 Did you know enough English to ask for your ticket?
   It wasn't necessary to say anything. I bought my ticket at a machine.
14 **It isn't necessary to** buy a licence for a bicycle in England. (*We . . .*)
15 **Is it essential for you to** finish tonight?
16 **Is it necessary for people to** go everywhere by boat in Venice?
17 **Will it be necessary for me to** sleep under a mosquito net?

18 Most people think that civil servants **are not required to** work very hard.
19 **It wasn't necessary to swim.** We were able to wade across.
20 **It isn't necessary for you to** drive me to the station. I can get a taxi.
21 Our plane was delayed so we had lunch at the airport. But **it wasn't necessary to** pay for the lunch. The airline gave it to us.
22 **Is it obligatory for us to** vote?
23 When you were a child **were you required to** practise the piano?
24 I saw the accident but fortunately **it wasn't necessary for me to** give evidence as there were plenty of other witnesses.
25 Small boy to friend: **It won't be necessary for you to** work hard when you come to my school. The teachers aren't very strict.
26 They had plenty of time. **It wasn't necessary for them to** hurry.
27 **Is it necessary for you to** take your dog with you everywhere?
٢3 What time **was it necessary for you to** leave home?
29 I brought my passport but I **wasn't required to** show it to anyone.
30 I missed one day of the exam. **Will it be necessary for me to** take the whole exam again?
31 **Is it really necessary for you to** practise the violin at 3 a.m.?
32 Everything was done for me. **It wasn't necessary for me to** do anything.
33 **Are** French children **obliged to** go to school on Saturdays?
34 I was late for the opera. ~
Was it necessary for you to wait till the end of the first act before finding your seat?
35 He repaired my old watch so **it wasn't necessary for me to** buy a new one after all.
36 **Were you required to** make a speech?

27 **must, can't** and **needn't** with the perfect infinitive

■ PEG 152, 156, 159

must + perfect infinitive is used for affirmative deductions.
can't/couldn't + infinitive is used for negative deductions.
needn't + perfect infinitive is used for a past action which was unnecessary but was performed.

Fill the spaces in the following sentences by using one of these forms + the perfect infinitive of the verbs in brackets.

1 Did you hear me come in last night? ~
No, I . . . (be) asleep.
2 I wonder who broke the wineglass; it . . . (be) the cat for she was out all day.
3 You . . . (help) him. (*You helped him but he didn't need help.*)

4 I had my umbrella when I came out but I haven't got it now. ~
You . . . (leave) it on the bus.
5 He . . . (escape) by this window because it is barred.
6 I . . . (give) £10. £5 would have been enough.
7 I saw a rattlesnake near the river yesterday. ~
You . . . (see) a rattlesnake. There aren't any rattlesnakes in this country.
8 He is back already. ~
He . . . (start) very early.
9 He returned home with a tiger cub. ~
His wife (be) very pleased about that.
10 I bought two bottles of milk. ~
You . . . (buy) milk; we have heaps in the house.
11 I phoned you at nine this morning but got no answer. ~
I'm sorry. I . . . (be) in the garden.
12 I left my bicycle here and now it's gone. ~
Someone . . . (borrow) it.
13 When she woke up her watch had vanished. ~
Someone . . . (steal) it while she slept.
14 I've opened another bottle. ~
You . . . (do) that. We've only just started this one.
15 The machine said, 'You weigh 65 kilos,' and I said, 'Thank you.' ~
You . . . (say) anything.
16 I told him to turn left and he immediately turned right! ~
He . . . (understand) you.
17 Perhaps he swam across. ~
No, he . . . (do) that; he can't swim.
18 Do you remember reading about it in the newspapers? ~
No, I . . . (be) abroad at the time.
19 He . . . (walk) from here to London in two hours. It isn't possible.
20 He was very sick last night. ~
The meat we had for supper . . . (be) good.
21 There was a dock strike and the liner couldn't leave port. ~
The passengers . . . (be) furious.
22 We went to a restaurant and had a very good dinner for £3. ~
You . . . (have) a very good dinner if you only paid £3.
23 I have just watered the roses. ~
You . . . (water) them. Look, it's raining now!
24 That carpet was made entirely by hand. ~
It . . . (take) a long time.
25 The door was open. ~
It . . . (be) open. I had locked it myself and the key was in my pocket.
26 He said that he watered the plants every day. ~
He . . . (water) them. If he had they wouldn't have died.
27 He came out of the water with little red spots all over his back. ~
He . . . (be) stung by a jelly-fish.

28 We've sent for a doctor. ~
    You . . . (send) for him. I am perfectly well.
29 I've made two copies. ~
    You . . . (make) two. One would have been enough.
30 There was a terrible crash at 3 a.m. ~
    That . . . (be) Tom coming in from his party.
31 I had to get down the mountain in a thick fog. ~
    That . . . (be) very difficult.
32 I saw Ann in the library yesterday. ~
    You . . . (see) her; she is still abroad.
33 How did he get out of the house? He . . . (come) down the stairs for
    they were blazing.
34 You . . . (lend) him your map. He has one of his own.
35 I spoke in English, very slowly. ~
    You . . . (speak) slowly. He speaks English very fluently.
36 He was found unconscious at the foot of the cliff. He . . . (fall) 200
    metres.

3 Present and past tenses

28 The simple present tense

☐ PEG 172

Read the following in the third person singular. Do not change the object if it is plural. Note that after certain consonants a final **es** is pronounced as a separate syllable. See PEG 12 B: *kiss, kisses* /kɪs, kɪsɪz/.

1 They wish to speak to you. (He)
2 Buses pass my house every hour.
3 They help their father. (He)
4 We change planes at Heathrow.
5 You watch too much TV. (He)
6 They worry too much. (He)
7 I cash a cheque every month. (He)
8 I always carry an umbrella. (She)
9 They wash the floor every week. (She)
10 His sons go to the local school.
11 These hens lay brown eggs.
12 Rubber balls bounce.
13 These figures astonish me.
14 Do you like boiled eggs? (he)
15 These seats cost £10.
16 They fish in the lake. (He)
17 Elephants never forget.
18 They usually catch the 8.10 bus.
19 They sometimes miss the bus.
20 I mix the ingredients together.
21 The rivers freeze in winter.
22 They fly from London to Edinburgh.
23 The carpets match the curtains.
24 They realize the danger.
25 I use a computer.
26 What do they do on their days off? ~
   They do nothing. They lie in bed all day.
27 The boys hurry home after school.
28 They push the door open.
29 They kiss their mother.
30 They box in the gymnasium.
31 They dress well.
32 Your children rely on you.

33 They snatch ladies' handbags.
34 You fry everything.
35 The taxes rise every year.
36 They do exercises every morning.

29 The simple present tense

□ PEG 172

Read the following (a) in the negative (b) in the interrogative.

In Nos. 2 and 14, **have** is used as an ordinary verb and should be treated as one.

1 You know the answer.
2 He has breakfast at 8.00.
3 He loves her.
4 Some schoolgirls wear uniforms.
5 He trusts you.
6 He tries hard.
7 The park closes at dusk.
8 He misses his mother.
9 The children like sweets.
10 He finishes work at 6.00.
11 He lives beside the sea.
12 He bullies his sisters.
13 This stove heats the water.
14 She has a cooked breakfast.
15 She carries a sleeping bag.
16 He usually believes you.
17 She dances in competitions.
18 You remember the address.
19 She plays chess very well.
20 He worries about her.
21 These thieves work at night.
22 He leaves home at 8.00 every day.
23 Ann arranges everything.
24 She agrees with you.
25 Their dogs bark all night.
26 Their neighbours often complain.
27 Tom enjoys driving at night.
28 He engages new staff every Spring.
29 Tom looks very well.
30 They sell fresh grape juice here.
31 He charges more than other photographers.
32 She cuts her husband's hair.
33 They pick the apples in October.
34 The last train leaves at midnight.

35 He relaxes at weekends.
36 She refuses to discuss it.

30 The present continuous tense

☐ PEG 164–7

Put the verbs in brackets into the present continuous tense. In No.
25, **have** is used as an ordinary verb and can therefore be used in the
continuous tense.

1 She (not work), she (swim) in the river.
2 He (teach) his boy to ride.
3 Why Ann (not wear) her new dress?
4 The aeroplane (fly) at 2,000 metres.
5 What Tom (do) now? He (clean) his shoes.
6 This fire (go) out. Somebody (bring) more coal?
7 It (rain)? ~
  Yes, it (rain) very hard. You can't go out yet.
8 Why you (mend) that old shirt?
9 You (not tell) the truth. ~
  How do you know that I (not tell) the truth?
10 Who (move) the furniture about upstairs? ~
  It's Tom. He (paint) the front bedroom.
11 Mrs Jones (sweep) the steps outside her house.
12 What you (read) now? I (read) *Crime and Punishment.*
13 It is a lovely day. The sun (shine) and the birds (sing).
14 Someone (knock) at the door. Shall I answer it? ~
  I (come) in a minute. I just (wash) my hands.
15 She always (ring) up and (ask) questions.
16 Why you (make) a cake? Someone (come) to tea?
17 Where is Tom? ~
  He (lie) under the car.
18 Can I borrow your pen or you (use) it at the moment?
19 You (do) anything this evening? ~
  No, I'm not. ~
  Well, I (go) to the cinema. Would you like to come with me?
20 We (have) breakfast at 8.00 tomorrow as Tom (catch) an early train.
21 Ann usually does the shopping, but I (do) it today as she isn't well.
22 Why you (type) so fast? You (make) a lot of mistakes.
23 Mother (rest) now. She always rests after lunch.
24 They (dig) an enormous hole just outside my gate. ~
  What they (do) that for? ~
  I don't know. Perhaps they (look) for oil.
25 What (make) that terrible noise? ~
  It's the pneumatic drill. They (repair) the road.

26 The children are very quiet. Go and see what they (do). ~
They (cut) up some £5 notes.
27 What you (wait) for? ~
I (wait) for my change; the boy just (get) it.
28 I can't hear what you (say); the traffic (make) too much noise.
29 She always (lose) her glasses and (ask) me to look for them.
30 Mother: What you (look) at? Something (happen) in the street?
31 Child: Yes. The house opposite is on fire! Come and look.
Mother: I can't. I (bath) the babies. Is the Fire Brigade here?
32 Child: Yes. Fire engines (rush) up and the firemen (jump) out and
(unroll) their hoses.
33 Smoke (pour) from the windows! People (stop) to watch.
A policeman (try) to move them on.
34 An old man (climb) out of a first floor window!
A fireman (help) him! Two boys (slide) down a rope!
35 A woman (wave) from the attic and a fireman (go) up a ladder to
help her!
36 Now he (come) down again! He (carry) a baby! The crowd (cheer!)

31 The simple present and the present continuous

▞ PEG 164–74

Put the verbs in brackets into the simple present or the present
continuous tense.

1 Cuckoos (not build) nests. They (use) the nests of other birds.
2 You can't see Tom now: he (have) a bath.
3 He usually (drink) coffee but today he (drink) tea.
4 What she (do) in the evenings? ~
She usually (play) cards or (watch) TV.
5 I won't go out now as it (rain) and I (not have) an umbrella.
6 The last train (leave) the station at 11.30.
7 He usually (speak) so quickly that I (not understand) him.
8 Ann (make) a dress for herself at the moment. She (make) all her
own clothes.
9 Hardly anyone (wear) a hat nowadays.
10 I'm afraid I've broken one of your coffee cups. ~
Don't worry. I (not like) that set anyway.
11 I (wear) my sunglasses today because the sun is very strong.
12 Tom can't have the newspaper now because his aunt (read) it.
13 I'm busy at the moment. I (redecorate) the sitting room.
14 The kettle (boil) now. Shall I make the tea?
15 You (enjoy) yourself or would you like to leave now? ~
I (enjoy) myself very much. I (want) to stay to the end.
16 How you (get) to work as a rule? ~
I usually (go) by bus but tomorrow I (go) in Tom's car.

17 Why you (put) on your coat? ~
    I (go) for a walk. You (come) with me? ~
    Yes, I'd love to come. You (mind) if I bring my dog?
18 How much you (owe) him? ~
    I (owe) him £5. ~
    You (intend) to pay him?
19 You (belong) to your local library? ~
    Yes, I do. ~
    You (read) a lot? ~
    Yes, quite a lot. ~
    How often you (change) your books? ~
    I (change) one every day.
20 Mary usually (learn) languages very quickly but she (not seem) able
    to learn modern Greek.
21 I always (buy) lottery tickets but I never (win) anything.
22 You (like) this necklace? I (give) it to my daughter for her birthday
    tomorrow.
23 I won't tell you my secret unless you (promise) not to tell anyone. ~
    I (promise).
24 You always (write) with your left hand?
25 You (love) him? ~
    No, I (like) him very much but I (not love) him.
26 You (dream) at night? ~
    Yes, I always (dream) and if I (eat) too much supper I (have)
    nightmares.
27 The milk (smell) sour. You (keep) milk a long time?
28 These workmen are never satisfied; they always (complain).
29 We (use) this room today because the window in the other room is
    broken.
30 He always (say) that he will mend the window but he never (do) it.
31 You (know) why an apple (fall) down and not up?
32 You (write) to him tonight? ~
    Yes, I always (write) to him on his birthday. You (want) to send any
    message?
33 Tom and Mr Pitt (have) a long conversation. I (wonder) what they
    (talk) about.
34 You (believe) all that the newspapers say? ~
    No, I (not believe) any of it. ~
    Then why you (read) newspapers?
35 This car (make) a very strange noise. You (think) it is all right? ~
    Oh, that noise (not matter). It always (make) a noise like that.
36 The fire (smoke) horribly. I can't see across the room. ~
    I (expect) that birds (build) a nest in the chimney. ~
    Why you (not put) wire across the tops of your chimneys? ~
    Tom (do) that sometimes but it (not seem) to make any difference.

32 The simple present and the present continuous

■ PEG 164–74

Put the verbs in brackets into the simple present or present
continuous tense.

1 What Tom (think) of the Budget? ~
   He (think) it most unfair. ~
   I (agree) with him.
2 What this one (cost)? ~
   It (cost) forty pence.
3 You (hear) the wind? It (blow) very strongly tonight.
4 You (see) my car keys anywhere? ~
   No, I (look) for them but I (not see) them.
5 He never (listen) to what you say. He always (think) about
   something else.
6 This book is about a man who (desert) his family and (go) to live on
   a Pacific island.
7 You (understand) what the lecturer is saying? ~
   No, I (not understand) him at all.
8 What you (have) for breakfast usually? ~
   I usually (eat) a carrot and (drink) a glass of cold water.
9 When the curtain (rise) we (see) a group of workers. They (picket) a
   factory gate.
10 Why you (walk) so fast today? You usually (walk) quite slowly. ~
   I (hurry) because I (meet) my mother at 4 o'clock and she (not like)
   to be kept waiting.
11 I (wish) that dog would lie down. He (keep) jumping up on my lap. ~
   I (think) he (want) to go for a walk.
12 You (recognize) that man? ~
   I (think) that I have seen him before but I (not remember) his name.
13 Look at that crowd. I (wonder) what they (wait) for.
14 This message has just arrived and the man (wait) in case you (want)
   to send a reply.
15 Stop! You (not see) the notice? ~
   I (see) it but I can't read it because I (not wear) my glasses. What it
   (say)? ~
   It (say) 'These premises are patrolled by guard dogs'.
16 She always (borrow) from me and she never (remember) to pay me
   back.
17 You (need) another blanket or you (feel) warm enough?
18 It (save) time if you (take) the path through the wood? ~
   No, it (not matter) which path you take.
19 I (save) up because I (go) abroad in July.
20 I (think) it is a pity you don't take more exercise. You (get) fat.
21 The plane that you (look) at now just (take) off for Paris.
22 Tom never (do) any work in the garden; he always (work) on his car.

23 What he (do) to his car now? ~
    I (think) he (polish) it.
24 That film (come) to the local cinema next week. You (want) to see it?
25 How Peter (get) on at school? ~
    Very well. He (seem) to like the life.
26 Why Mrs Pitt (look) so angry? ~
    Mr Pitt (smoke) a cigarette and (drop) the ash on the carpet.
27 This is our itinerary. We (leave) home on the 8th, (arrive) in Paris on
    the 9th, (spend) the day in Paris, and (set) out that night for
    Venice. ~
    That (sound) most interesting. You must tell me all about it when
    you (get) back.
28 This story is about a boy who (make) friends with a snake which he
    (find) in his garden. Then he (go) away but he (not forget) the snake
    and some years later he (return) and (look) for it.
29 He (find) the snake who (recognize) its old friend and (coil) round
    him affectionately. But, unfortunately, the snake is by now a full-
    grown boa-constrictor and its embrace (kill) the poor boy.
30 The snake (feel) sorry about this? ~
    I (not know). The story (end) there.
31 How you (end) a letter that (begin), 'Dear Sir'? ~
    I always (put), 'Yours truly', but Tom (prefer) 'Yours faithfully'.
32 What the word 'catastrophe' (mean)? ~
    It (mean) 'disaster'.
33 What you (wait) for? ~
    I (wait) for the shop to open. ~
    But it (not open) till 9.00. ~
    I (know) but I (want) to be early, as their sale (start) today.
34 Why you (smoke) a cigar, Mrs Pitt? You (not smoke) cigars as a
    rule. ~
    I (smoke) it because I (want) the ash. This book (say) that cigar ash
    mixed with oil (remove) heat stains from wood.
35 Who (own) this umbrella? ~
    I (not know). Everybody (use) it but nobody (know) who (own) it.
36 You (mind) if I (ask) you a question? ~
    That (depend) on the question. ~
    It (concern) your brother. ~
    I (refuse) to answer any question about my brother.

33 The simple past tense

☐ PEG 175–6

Put the verbs in the following sentences into the simple past tense.

1 I go to work by bus.
2 I meet her on Tuesdays.

3 He always wears black.
4 I make cakes every week.
5 She gets up at 6.30.
6 He understands me.
7 He shuts the shop at 6.00.
8 She speaks slowly.
9 He leaves the house at 9.00.
10 I read a chapter every night.
11 You eat too much.
12 I see him every day.
13 Tom sings in the choir.
14 He cries when he is hurt.
15 Who knows the answer?
16 I think I know it.
17 The curtain rises at 8.00.
18 He takes the dog out twice a day.
19 We buy them here.
20 I dream every night.
21 Bluetits often lay eggs in that nesting box.
22 He often feels ill.
23 I know what he wants.
24 I usually pay him £5.
25 His dog always bites me.
26 It smells odd.
27 It costs 30p.
28 My back hurts.
29 I lie down after lunch.
30 We drink water.
31 His roses grow well.
32 He rides every day.
33 He often falls off.
34 These dogs fight whenever they meet.
35 He puts up his prices every year.
36 He sleeps badly.

34 The simple past tense

☐ PEG 175–6

Put the verbs in the following sentences into (a) the negative (b) the interrogative.

1 She saw your brother.
2 We heard a terrible noise.
3 He slept till 10.00.
4 He looked at the picture.
5 They drank all the wine.

6 They set out early enough.
7 She thought about it.
8 The police caught the thief.
9 He hid the letter.
10 She found her watch.
11 His nose bled.
12 My mother chose this hotel.
13 She lent you enough money.
14 Keiko taught Japanese.
15 Tom hurt his foot.
16 He broke his arm.
17 His wife came at 8.00.
18 He lost his wallet.
19 His son wrote a novel.
20 They flew to New York.
21 Ann drew you a map.
22 Tom laid the table.
23 Mr Pitt fell downstairs.
24 She lost her way.
25 He forbade her to leave.
26 I sent it to the laundry.
27 Jack kept the money.
28 He rode slowly.
29 They spent it all.
30 She sold the car.
31 Jean rang the bell.
32 The sun rose at 6.00.
33 The boys ran home.
34 He shook the bottle.
35 He forgave her.
36 They broadcast an appeal for money.

35 The past continuous tense

☐ PEG 178

Put the verbs in brackets into the past continuous tense.

1 Detective: I'm afraid I must ask you both what you (do) yesterday at
10.20 p.m.
Mr X: I (play) chess with my wife.
Mr Y: I (listen) to a play on the radio.
2 The children were frightened because it (get) dark.
3 It was a fine day and the roads were crowded because a lot of people
(rush) to the seaside.
4 The aeroplane in which the football team (travel) crashed soon after
taking off.

Present and past tenses

5 He usually wears sandals but when I last saw him he (wear) boots.
6 The house was in great disorder because he (redecorate) it.
7 The director didn't allow the actors to travel by air while they (work) on the film.
8 The car had nobody in it but the engine (run).
9 Two children (play) on the sand and two fishermen (lean) against an upturned boat.
10 I was alone in the house at that time because Mr Jones (work) in the garage and Mrs Jones (shop).
11 He said that he was the captain of a ship which (sail) that night for Marseilles.
12 Are you going to Rome? I thought that you (go) to Milan.
13 My wife and I (talk) about you the other day.
14 When I first met him he (study) painting.
15 There was a strong smell and the sound of frying. Obviously Mrs Jones (cook) fish.
16 Tom ate nothing for lunch because he (diet). He said that he (try) to lose 10 kilos.
17 Who you (talk) to on the telephone as I came in?
   I (talk) to Mr Pitt.
18 As she (climb) the ladder it slipped sideways and she fell off it.
19 When I first met him he (work) in a restaurant.
20 He watched the children for a moment. Some of them (bathe) in the sea, others (look) for shells, others (play) in the sand.
21 Where he (live) when you saw him last?
22 She (stand) at the bus stop. I asked her what bus she (wait) for.
23 From the sounds it was clear that Mary (practise) the piano.
24 There had been an accident and men (carry) the injured people to an ambulance.
25 Two men (fight) at a street corner and a policeman (try) to stop them. ~
   What they (fight) about? ~
   Nobody seemed to know.
26 Tom (sit) in a corner with a book. I told him that he (read) in very bad light.
27 I went into the garden to see what the boys (do). James (weed) and Alexander (cut) the grass.
28 They had taken off the wheel of the car and (mend) the puncture. I asked when it would be ready.
29 When I arrived at the meeting the first speaker had just finished speaking and the audience (clap).
30 The traffic (make) so much noise that I couldn't hear what he (say).
31 While he (learn) to drive he had twenty-five accidents.
32 He had a bad fall while he (repair) his roof.
33 He was a little mad. He always (try) to prove that the earth was flat.
34 While we (fish) someone came to the house and left this note.

35 The exam had just begun and the candidates (write) their names at the top of their papers.
36 Just as I (wonder) what to do next, the phone rang.

36 The simple past and the past continuous

☐ PEG 175–81

Put the verbs in brackets into the simple past or the past continuous tense.

1 I lit the fire at 6.00 and it (burn) brightly when Tom came in at 7.00.
2 When I arrived the lecture had already started and the professor (write) on the overhead projector.
3 I (make) a cake when the light went out. I had to finish it in the dark.
4 I didn't want to meet Paul so when he entered the room I (leave).
5 Unfortunately when I arrived Ann just (leave), so we only had time for a few words.
6 He (watch) TV when the phone rang. Very unwillingly he (turn) down the sound and (go) to answer it.
7 He was very polite. Whenever his wife entered the room he (stand) up.
8 The admiral (play) bowls when he received news of the invasion. He (insist) on finishing the game.
9 My dog (walk) along quietly when Mr Pitt's Pekinese attacked him.
10 When I arrived she (have) lunch. She apologized for starting without me but said that she always (lunch) at 12.30.
11 He always (wear) a raincoat and (carry) an umbrella when he walked to the office.
12 What you (think) of his last book? ~
I (like) it very much.
13 I (share) a flat with him when we were students. He always (complain) about my untidiness.
14 He suddenly (realize) that he (travel) in the wrong direction.
15 He (play) the guitar outside her house when someone opened the window and (throw) out a bucket of water.
16 I just (open) the letter when the wind (blow) it out of my hand.
17 The burglar (open) the safe when he (hear) footsteps. He immediately (put) out his torch and (crawl) under the bed.
18 When I (look) for my passport I (find) this old photograph.
19 You looked very busy when I (see) you last night. What you (do)?
20 The boys (play) cards when they (hear) their father's step. They immediately (hide) the cards and (take) out their lesson books.
21 He (clean) his gun when it accidentally (go) off and (kill) him.
22 He (not allow) us to go out in the boat yesterday as a strong wind (blow).

23 As I (cross) the road I (step) on a banana skin and (fall) heavily.
24 I still (lie) on the road when I (see) a lorry approaching.
25 Luckily the driver (see) me and (stop) the lorry in time.
26 How you (damage) your car so badly? ~
I (run) into a lamp-post yesterday. ~
I suppose you (drive) too quickly or were not looking where you (go).
27 As he (get) into the bus it (start) suddenly and he (fall) backwards on
to the road.
28 I (call) Paul at 7.00 but it wasn't necessary because he already (get)
up.
29 When he (mend) the fuse he (get) a very bad shock.
30 When I (hear) his knock I (go) to the door and (open) it, but I (not
recognize) him at first because I (not wear) my glasses.
31 When I came in they (sit) round the fire. Mr Pitt (do) a crossword
puzzle, Mrs Pitt (knit), the others (read). Mrs Pitt (smile) at me and
(say), 'Come and sit down.'
32 While the guests (dance) thieves (break) into the house and (steal) a
lot of fur coats.
33 The next day, as they (know) that the police (look) for them, they
(hide) the coats in a wood and (go) off in different directions.
34 She was very extravagant. She always (buy) herself new clothes.
35 Her mother often (tell) her that she (spend) too much money but she
never (listen).
36 Whenever the drummer (begin) practising, the people in the next flat
(bang) on the wall.

37 The simple past and the past continuous

■ PEG 175–81

Put the verbs in brackets into the simple past or past continuous
tense.

1 Mr Smith never (wake) up in time in the mornings and always (get)
into trouble for being late; so one day he (go) to town and (buy) an
alarm clock.
2 To get home he (have to) go through a field where a bad-tempered
bull usually (graze).
3 This bull normally (not chase) people unless something (make) him
angry. Unfortunately, as Mr Smith (cross) the field, his alarm clock
(go) off.
4 This (annoy) the bull, who immediately (begin) to chase Mr Smith.
5 Mr Smith (carry) an open umbrella as it (rain) slightly. He (throw)
the umbrella to the ground and (run) away as fast as he could.
6 The bull (stop) and (begin) to attack the umbrella. While he (do) this
Mr Smith escaped.

7 When he (awake) she (sit) by the window. She (look) at something in the street, but when he (call) her she (turn) and (smile) at him.

8 Why you (interrupt) me just now? I (have) a very interesting conversation with Mr Pitt.

9 The murderer (carry) the corpse down the stairs when he (hear) a knock on the door.

10 When I (look) through your books I (notice) that you have a copy of *Murder in the Cathedral.*

11 As they (walk) along the road they (hear) a car coming from behind them. Tom (turn) round and (hold) up his hand. The car (stop).

12 When I (arrive) at the station Mary (wait) for me. She (wear) a blue dress and (look) very pretty. As soon as she (see) me she (wave) and (shout) something, but I couldn't hear what she (say) because everybody (make) such a noise.

13 The prisoner (escape) by climbing the wall of the garden where he (work). He (wear) blue overalls and black shoes.

14 She said that the car (travel) at 40 k.p.h. when it (begin) to skid.

15 She said that she (not like) her present flat and (try) to find another.

16 While he (make) his speech the minister suddenly (feel) faint. But someone (bring) him a glass of water and after a few minutes he (be able) to continue.

17 When I (see) him he (paint) a portrait of his wife. ~
You (like) it? ~
He only just (start) when I (see) it, so I couldn't judge.

18 I (take) my friend to a murder trial the other day. ~
Who (be) tried? ~
A man called Bill Sykes. ~
Was he acquitted? ~
I don't know. They still (listen) to the evidence when we (leave).

19 I (be) sorry that I (have to) leave the party early, because I (enjoy) myself.

20 As we (come) here a policeman (stop) us. He (say) that he (look) for some stolen property and (ask) if he could search the car.

21 I (see) you yesterday from the bus. Why you (use) a stick? ~
I (use) a stick because I had hurt my leg that morning falling off a horse. ~
Whose horse you (ride)?

22 The floor was covered with balls of wool. Obviously Mrs Pitt (knit) something.

23 Ann said that she (be) on holiday. I (say) that I (hope) that she (enjoy) herself.

24 While he (water) the flowers it (begin) to rain. He (put) up his umbrella and (go) on watering.

25 I just (write) a cheque when I (remember) that I (have) nothing in the bank.

26 I (find) this ring as I (dig) in the garden. It looks very old. I wonder who it (belong) to?

27 When I last (see) her she (hurry) along the road to the station. I (ask) her where she (go) and she (say), 'London', but I don't think she (speak) the truth because there (not be) any train for London at that time.

28 The tailor said, 'Your suit will be ready on Monday.' But when I (call) on Monday he still (work) on it.

29 The teacher (come) into the classroom unusually early and one of the boys, who (smoke) a cigarette, (have) no time to put it out. So he (throw) it into the desk and (hope) for the best.

30 A little later the teacher (notice) that smoke (rise) from this desk. 'You (smoke) when I (come) in?' he (ask).

31 While I (swim) someone (steal) my clothes and I (have to) walk home in my swimsuit.

32 The men (say) that they (work) on the road outside my house and that they (want) some water to make tea.

33 He (say) that he (build) himself a house and that he (think) it would be ready in two years.

34 At 3 a.m. Mrs Pitt (wake) her husband and (say) that she (think) that someone (try) to get into the house.

35 Why you (lend) him that book? I still (read) it. ~
I'm sorry. I (not know) that you still (read) it.

36 I (come) in very late last night and unfortunately the dog (wake) up and (start) to bark. This (wake) my mother who (come) to the top of the stairs and (say), 'Who is there?'
I (say), 'It is me,' but she (not hear) me because the dog (bark) so loudly, so she (go) back to her room and (telephone) the police.

38 The present perfect tense

☐ PEG 182–9

Put the verbs in brackets into the present perfect tense, and fill the spaces by repeating the auxiliary.

You (wash) the plates? ~
Yes, I ... .
Have you washed the plates? ~
Yes, I have.

You (see) him lately? ~
No, I ...
Have you seen him lately? ~
No, I haven't.

1 Where you (be)? ~
I (be) to the dentist.

2 You (have) breakfast? ~
Yes, I ...

3 The post (come)? ~
Yes, it . . .
4 You (see) my watch anywhere? ~
No, I'm afraid I . . .
5 Someone (wind) the clock? ~
Yes, Tom . . .
6 I (not finish) my letter yet.
7 He just (go) out.
8 Someone (take) my bicycle.
9 The phone (stop) ringing.
10 You (hear) from her lately? ~
No, I . . .
11 I just (wash) that floor.
12 The cat (steal) the fish.
13 You (explain) the exercise? ~
Yes, I . . .
14 There aren't any buses because the drivers (go) on strike.
15 You (have) enough to eat? ~
Yes, I (have) plenty, thank you.
16 Charles (pass) his exam? ~
Yes, he . . .
17 How many bottles the milkman (leave)? ~
He (leave) six.
18 I (live) here for ten years.
19 How long you (know) Mr Pitt? ~
I (know) him for ten years.
20 Would you like some coffee? I just (make) some.
21 Mary (water) the tomatoes? ~
Yes, I think she . . .
22 You (not make) a mistake? ~
No, I'm sure I . . .
23 Why you (not mend) the fuse? ~
I (not have) time.
24 You (dive) from the ten-metre board yet? ~
No, I . . .
25 You ever (leave) a restaurant without paying the bill? ~
No, I . . .
26 I (ask) him to dinner several times.
27 He always (refuse).
28 You ever (ride) a camel?
29 I (buy) a new carpet. Come and look at it.
30 He (post) the letter?
31 Why he (not finish)? He (have) plenty of time.
32 I often (see) him but I never (speak) to him.
33 You ever (eat) caviar? ~
No, I . . .
34 We just (hear) the most extraordinary news.

35 The police (recapture) the prisoners who escaped yesterday.
36 I (not pay) the telephone bill yet.

39 The present perfect and the simple past
☐ PEG 175-7, 182-9

(a) Fill the spaces by repeating the auxiliary used in the question, putting it into the negative where necessary.

(b) Put the verb in brackets into the present perfect or the simple past tense.

Have you seen that play? (a) Yes, I . . .
Yes, I have.

(b) Yes, I (be) there last night.
Yes, I was there last night.

1 Have you wound the clock?
(a) Yes, I . . .
(b) Yes, I (wind) it on Monday.

2 Have you ever eaten snails?
(a) No, I . . .
(b) Yes, I (eat) some at Tom's party last week.

3 Has she fed the dog?
(a) Yes, I think she . . .
(b) Yes, she (feed) him before lunch.

4 Have they repaired the road?
(a) No, they . . .
(b) They only (repair) part of it so far.

5 Have they done their homework?
(a) Yes, they (do) it all.
(b) Yes, they (do) it before they left school.

6 Have you found the matches?
(a) No, I . . .
(b) No, I (not find) them yet.

7 Have you made the coffee?
(a) Yes, I . . .
(b) I (make) some yesterday: we can use that.

8 Have you been here before?
(a) No, I . . .
(b) Yes, I (be) here several times.

9 Have you seen him lately?
(a) No, I . . .
(b) No, I (not see) him since Christmas.

10 Have you been to the opera this week?
(a) Yes, I . . .
(b) Yes, I (go) to *Faust* on Friday.

11 Have you ever driven this car?

  (a) Yes, I (drive) it once or twice.
  (b) Yes, I (drive) it when you were away.

12 Has he missed his train?

  (a) No, he . . . .
  (b) Yes, he . . . It (go) five minutes ago.

13 Have they been through Customs?

  (a) Yes, they . . .
  (b) Yes, their luggage (be) examined at Dover.

14 Has he spoken to her?

  (a) Yes, he . . .
  (b) Yes, he (speak) to her on Friday.

15 Have you spent all your money?

  (a) No, I only (spend) half of it.
  (b) Yes, I . . .

16 How much have you saved since Christmas?

  (a) I (not save) anything.
  (b) I (save) £3.

17 Has his temperature gone down?

  (a) No, it . . .
  (b) Yes, it (go) down last night.

18 Have you seen his garden?

  (a) No, I (not see) it yet.
  (b) I (see) the house on Monday but I (not see) the garden.

19 Have you paid the bill?

  (a) Yes, I . . .
  (b) Yes, I (pay) it while you were away.

20 Have you ever flown a plane?

  (a) No, I . . .
  (b) Yes, I (fly) when I was at university.

21 Has your dog ever bitten anyone?

  (a) Yes, he (bite) a policeman last week.
  (b) Yes, he (bite) me twice.

22 Have you planted your peas?

  (a) Yes, I (plant) them on Tuesday.
  (b) No, I . . . yet.

23 Has he written to the paper?

  (a) Yes, he . . .
  (b) Yes, he (write) at once.

24 Have you ever drunk vodka?

  (a) No, I . . .
  (b) I (drink) it once in Russia but I (not drink) it since.

40 The present perfect and the simple past

■ PEG 175–7, 182–9

Put the verbs in brackets into the present perfect or the simple past tense. In some sentences the present perfect continuous (PEG 190) is also possible.

1 This is my house. ~
How long you (live) here? ~
I (live) here since 1970.
2 He (live) in London for two years and then (go) to Edinburgh.
3 You (wear) your hair long when you were at school? ~
Yes, my mother (insist) on it.
4 But when I (leave) school I (cut) my hair and (wear) it short ever since.
5 Shakespeare (write) a lot of plays.
6 My brother (write) several plays. He just (finish) his second tragedy.
7 I (fly) over Loch Ness last week. ~
You (see) the Loch Ness monster?
8 I (not see) him for three years. I wonder where he is.
9 He (not smoke) for two weeks. He is trying to give it up.
10 Chopin (compose) some of his music in Majorca.
11 When he (arrive)? ~
He (arrive) at 2.00.
12 You (lock) the door before you left the house?
13 I (read) his books when I was at school. I (enjoy) them very much.
14 I can't go out because I (not finish) my work.
15 I never (drink) whisky. ~
Well, have some now.
16 I (write) the letter but I can't find a stamp.
17 The clock is slow. ~
It isn't slow, it (stop).
18 Here are your shoes; I just (clean) them.
19 I (leave) home at 8.00 and (get) here at twelve.
20 I (do) this sort of work when I (be) an apprentice.
21 He just (go) out.
22 He (go) out ten minutes ago.
23 You (have) breakfast yet? ~
Yes, I (have) it at 8.00.
24 I (meet) him last June.
25 You (see) the moon last night?
26 The concert (begin) at 2.30 and (last) for two hours. Everyone (enjoy) it very much.
27 The play just (begin). You are a little late.
28 The newspaper (come)? ~
Yes, Ann is reading it.

29 The actors (arrive) yesterday and (start) rehearsals early this morning.
30 It (be) very cold this year. I wonder when it is going to get warmer.
31 Cervantes (write) *Don Quixote.*
32 We (miss) the bus. Now we'll have to walk.
33 He (break) his leg in a skiing accident last year.
34 Mr Pound is the bank manager. He (be) here for five years.
35 Mr Count (work) as a cashier for twenty-five years. Then he (retire) and (go) to live in the country.
36 You (be) here before? ~
Yes, I (spend) my holidays here last year. ~
You (have) a good time? ~
No, it never (stop) raining.

41 The present perfect and the simple past

■ PEG 175–7, 182–9

Put the verbs in brackets into the present perfect or simple past tense. Fill the spaces by repeating the auxiliary used in the preceding verb.
    You (see) Mary on Monday? ~
    Yes, I . . .
    Did you see Mary on Monday? ~
    Yes, I did.

1 Where is Tom? ~
I (not see) him today, but he (tell) Mary that he'd be in for dinner.
2 I (buy) this in Bond Street. ~
How much you (pay) for it? ~
I (pay) £100.
3 Where you (find) this knife? ~
I (find) it in the garden. ~
Why you (not leave) it there?
4 I (lose) my black gloves. You (see) them anywhere? ~
No, I'm afraid I . . . . When you last (wear) them? ~
I (wear) them at the theatre last night. ~
Perhaps you (leave) them at the theatre.
5 Do you know that lady who just (leave) the shop? ~
Yes, that is Miss Thrift. Is she a customer of yours? ~
Not exactly. She (be) in here several times but she never (buy) anything.
6 He (leave) the house at 8.00. ~
Where he (go)? ~
I (not see) where he (go).

7 He (serve) in the First World War. ~
When that war (begin)? ~
It (begin) in 1914 and (last) for four years.

8 Who you (vote) for at the last election? ~
I (vote) for Mr Pitt. ~
He (not be) elected, (be) he? ~
No, he (lose) his deposit.

9 You (like) your last job? ~
I (like) it at first but then I (quarrel) with my employer and he (dismiss) me. ~
How long you (be) there? ~
I (be) there for two weeks.

10 I (not know) that you (know) Mrs Pitt. How long you (know) her? ~
I (know) her for ten years.

11 That is Mr Minus, who teaches me mathematics, but he (not have) time to teach me much. I only (be) in his class for a week.

12 You (hear) his speech on the radio last night? ~
Yes, I . . . ~
What you (think) of it?

13 I (not know) that you (be) here. You (be) here long? ~
Yes, I (be) here two months. ~
You (be) to the Cathedral? ~
Yes, I (go) there last Sunday.

14 You ever (try) to give up smoking? ~
Yes, I (try) last year, but then I (find) that I was getting fat so I (start) again.

15 You (see) today's paper? ~
No, anything interesting (happen)?
Yes, two convicted murderers (escape) from the prison down the road.

16 Mary (feed) the cat? ~
Yes, she (feed) him before lunch. ~
What she (give) him? ~
She (give) him some fish.

17 How long you (know) your new assistant? ~
I (know) him for two years. ~
What he (do) before he (come) here? ~
I think he (be) in prison.

18 I (not see) your aunt recently. ~
No. She (not be) out of her house since she (buy) her colour TV.

19 The plumber (be) here yet? ~
Yes, but he only (stay) for an hour. ~
What he (do) in that time? ~
He (turn) off the water and (empty) the tank.

20 Where you (be)?
   I (be) out in a yacht. ~
   You (enjoy) it? ~
   Yes, very much. We (take) part in a race. ~
   You (win)? ~
   No, we (come) in last.
21 How long that horrible monument (be) there? ~
   It (be) there six months. Lots of people (write) to the Town Council
   asking them to take it away but so far nothing (be) done.
22 I just (be) to the film *War and Peace*. You (see) it? ~
   No, I . . . . Is it like the book? ~
   I (not read) the book. ~
   I (read) it when I (be) at school. ~
   When Tolstoy (write) it? ~
   He (write) it in 1868. ~
   He (write) anything else?
23 Hannibal (bring) elephants across the Alps. ~
   Why he (do) that? ~
   He (want) to use them in battle.
24 Where you (be)? ~
   I (be) to the dentist. ~
   He (take) out your bad tooth? ~
   Yes, he . . . ~
   It (hurt)? ~
   Yes, horribly.
25 She (say) that she'd phone me this morning, but it is now 12.30 and
   she (not phone) yet.
26 I just (receive) a letter saying that we (not pay) this quarter's
   electricity bill. I (not give) you the money for that last week? ~
   Yes, you . . . but I'm afraid I (spend) it on something else.
27 How long you (be) out of work? ~
   I'm not out of work now. I just (start) a new job. ~
   How you (find) the job? ~
   I (answer) an advertisement in the paper.
28 You (finish) checking the accounts? ~
   No, not quite. I (do) about half so far.
29 I (cut) my hand rather badly. Have you a bandage? ~
   I'll get you one. How it (happen)? ~
   I was chopping some wood and the axe (slip).
30 How you (get) that scar? ~
   I (get) it in a car accident a year ago.
31 You (meet) my brother at the lecture yesterday? ~
   Yes, I . . . . We (have) coffee together afterwards.
32 He (lose) his job last month and since then he (be) out of work. ~
   Why he (lose) his job? ~
   He (be) very rude to Mr Pitt.

33 What are all those people looking at? ~
There (be) an accident. ~
You (see) what (happen)? ~
Yes, a motor cycle (run) into a lorry.

34 I (phone) you twice yesterday and (get) no answer.

35 Originally horses used in bull fights (not wear) any protection, but for some time now they (wear) special padding.

36 That house (be) empty for a year. But they just (take) down the 'For Sale' sign, so I suppose someone (buy) it.

42 The present perfect continuous tense

□ PEG 190-1

Put the verbs in brackets into the present perfect continuous tense.

1 I (make) cakes. That is why my hands are all covered with flour.

2 Her phone (ring) for ten minutes. I wonder why she doesn't answer it.

3 He (overwork). That is why he looks so tired.

4 There is sawdust in your hair. ~
I'm not surprised. I (cut) down a tree.

5 Have you seen my bag anywhere? I (look) for it for ages.

6 What you (do)? ~
I (work) in the laboratory.

7 He (study) Russian for two years and doesn't even know the alphabet yet.

8 How long you (wait) for me? ~
I (wait) about half an hour.

9 It (rain) for two days now. There'll be a flood soon.

10 We (argue) about this for two hours now. Perhaps we should stop!

11 I (bathe). That's why my hair is all wet.

12 You (drive) all day. Let me drive now.

13 How long you (wear) glasses?

14 The petrol gauge (say) 'Empty' for quite a long time now. Don't you think we should get some petrol?

15 I'm sorry for keeping you waiting. I (try) to make a telephone call to Rome.

16 You (not eat) enough lately. That's why you feel irritable.

17 He (speak) for an hour now. I expect he'll soon be finished.

18 That helicopter (fly) round the house for the last hour; do you think it's taking photographs?

19 The radio (play) since 7 a.m. I wish someone would turn it off.

20 I (shop) all day and I haven't a penny left.

21 We (live) here since 1977.

22 I'm on a diet. I (eat) nothing but bananas for the last month.

23 The children (look) forward to this holiday for months.

24 That pipe (leak) for ages. We must get it mended.
25 Tom (dig) in the garden all afternoon and I (help) him.
26 I (ask) you to mend that window for six weeks. When are you going
    to do it?
27 Someone (use) my bicycle. The chain's fallen off.
28 How long you (drive)? ~
    I (drive) for ten years.
29 The trial (go) on for a long time. I wonder what the verdict will be.
30 It (snow) for three days now. The roads will be blocked if it doesn't
    stop soon.
31 Mary (cry)? ~
    No, she (not cry), she (peel) onions.
32 The car (make) a very curious noise ever since it ran out of oil.
33 He walked very unsteadily up the stairs and his wife said, 'You
    (drink)!'
34 Your fingers are very brown. You (smoke) too much.
35 You usually know when someone (eat) garlic.
36 Ever since he came to us that man (try) to make trouble.

43 The present perfect and the present perfect continuous

◢ PEG 191–2

Put the verbs in brackets into the present perfect or the present
perfect continuous tense. (In some cases either could be used.)

1 We (walk) ten kilometres.
2 We (walk) for three hours.
3 You (walk) too fast. That's why you are tired.
4 I (make) sausage rolls for the party all the morning.
5 How many you (make)? ~
   I (make) 200.
6 That boy (eat) seven ice-creams.
7 He (not stop) eating since he arrived.
8 The driver (drink). I think someone else ought to drive.
9 I (pull) up 100 dandelions.
10 I (pull) up dandelions all day.
11 What you (do)? ~
    We (pick) apples.
12 How many you (pick)? ~
    We (pick) ten basketfuls.
13 I (sleep) on every bed in this house and I don't like any of them.
14 He (sleep) since ten o'clock. It's time he woke up.
15 He (ride); that's why he is wearing breeches.
16 I (ride) all the horses in this stable.
17 What a lovely smell! ~
    Mary (make) jam.

18 The students (work) very well this term.
19 I only (hear) from him twice since he went away.
20 I (hear) from her regularly. She is a very good correspondent.
21 I (grease) my car. That's why my hands are so dirty.
22 I (polish) this table all the morning and she isn't satisfied with it yet.
23 I (work) for him for ten years and he never once (say) 'Good morning' to me.
24 He (teach) in this school for five years.
25 I (teach) hundreds of students but I never (meet) such a hopeless class as this.
26 Why you (be) so long in the garage? ~
   The tyres were flat; I (pump) them up.
27 I (pump) up three tyres. Would you like to do the fourth?
28 I (look) for mushrooms but I (not find) any.
29 He (cough) a lot lately. He ought to give up smoking.
30 You (hear) the news? Tom and Ann are engaged! ~
   That's not new; I (know) it for ages!
31 I (try) to finish this letter for the last half-hour. I wish you'd go away or stop talking. ~
   I hardly (say) anything.
32 The driver of that car (sound) his horn for the last ten minutes.
33 It (rain) for two hours and the ground is too wet to play on, so the match (be) postponed.
34 He (hope) for a rise in salary for six months but he (not dare) to ask for it yet.
35 Mr Smith, you (whisper) to the student on your right for the last five minutes. You (help) him with his exam paper or he (help) you?
36 Why you (make) such a horrible noise? ~
   I (lose) my key and I (try) to wake my wife by throwing stones at her window. ~
   You (throw) stones at the wrong window. You live next door.

44 for and since

□ PEG 187

Fill the spaces in the following sentences by using **for** or **since**.

1 We've been fishing . . . two hours.
2 I've been working in this office . . . a month.
3 They've been living in France . . . 1970.
4 He has been in prison . . . a year.
5 I've known that . . . a long time.
6 That man has been standing there . . . six o'clock.
7 She has driven the same car . . . 1975.
8 Things have changed . . . I was a girl.
9 The kettle has been boiling . . . a quarter of an hour.

10 The central heating has been on . . . October.
11 That trunk has been in the hall . . . a year.
12 He has been very ill . . . the last month.
13 I've been using this machine . . . twelve years.
14 We've been waiting . . . half an hour.
15 Mr Pitt has been in hospital . . . his accident.
16 He hasn't spoken to me . . . the last committee meeting.
17 I have been very patient with you . . . several years.
18 They have been on strike . . . November.
19 The strike has lasted . . . six months.
20 It has been very foggy . . . early morning.
21 They have been quarrelling ever . . . they got married.
22 I've been awake . . . four o'clock.
23 I've been awake . . . a long time.
24 We've had no gas . . . the strike began.
25 I've earned my own living . . . I left school.
26 Nobody has seen him . . . last week.
27 The police have been looking for me . . . four days.
28 I haven't worn low-heeled shoes . . . I was at school.
29 He had a bad fall last week and . . . then he hasn't left the house.
30 He has been under water . . . half an hour.
31 That tree has been there . . . 2,000 years.
32 He has been Minister of Education . . . 1983.
33 I've been trying to open this door . . . forty-five minutes.
34 He hasn't eaten anything . . . twenty-four hours.
35 We've had terrible weather . . . the last month.
36 Nobody has come to see us . . . we bought these bloodhounds.

4 Future forms

45 The present continuous tense as a future form

☐ PEG 202

Put the verbs in brackets into the present continuous tense.

1 They are going to drill for oil here. They (start) on Monday.
2 My uncle (make) a speech on Friday.
3 I (take) my sister to the ballet tomorrow.
4 She (call) for me at six.
5 He (play) at Wimbledon next summer.
6 I (meet) her at the station at ten.
7 The sales (not start) till Monday.
8 How you (get) to the party tomorrow? ~
   I (go) by car. ~
   Who (drive)?
9 The piano tuner (come) this afternoon.
10 You (give) him anything for his birthday? ~
    Yes, I (give) him a dictionary.
11 The windows (be) cleaned today. Then we'll be able to see out.
12 She (come) out of hospital next week.
13 We (have) dinner early tonight as we (go) to the theatre.
14 Where you (go) for your holidays this year? ~
    I (go) to Holland.
15 He (not give) a lecture tonight.
16 I (have) my photograph taken tomorrow.
17 I (buy) her a burglar alarm for a wedding present.
18 The elections (be) held next week.
19 I (have) lunch with my aunt on Thursday.
20 The committee (meet) next Wednesday.
21 My grandparents (celebrate) their golden wedding next week.
22 I (lend) him my car for his holidays.
23 The strikers (return) to work next week.
24 Smith's (open) a new branch in this street in July.
25 We've bought a new house and (move) in very soon.
26 I (not take) up judo next winter.
27 They (get) married next week.
28 You (do) anything tonight? ~
    Yes, I (go) to my carpentry class.
29 The Prime Minister (fly) to America tomorrow.
30 He (start) a new job on Friday.

31 The Queen (give) a garden party next week. You (go)?
32 My brother (be) released on Tuesday. I (meet) him outside the prison.
33 I (catch) the 6.30 plane tomorrow. ~
Where you (leave) your car? ~
I (not take) the car.
34 Her mother (send) her to France next year.
35 I (go) to the dentist tomorrow. Miss Pitt (take) my class.
36 I (lend) my flat to my American cousins next year.

46 The **be going to** form

☐ PEG 203, 206

Put the verbs in brackets into the **be going to** form.

1 You (miss) your train.
2 The pressure cooker (explode).
3 When you (pay) the bill?
4 She (dye) the old curtains blue.
5 We (make) this whisky bottle into a lamp.
6 What you (do) with this room? ~
I (paint) the walls in black and white stripes.
7 The umpire (blow) his whistle.
8 You (eat) all that?
9 That man with the tomato in his hand (throw) it at the speaker.
10 That door (slam).
11 The bull (attack) us.
12 It (rain). Look at those clouds.
13 The cat (have) kittens.
14 The men in the helicopter (try) to rescue the man in the water.
15 That rider (fall) off.
16 These two men (cycle) across Africa.
17 The Lord Mayor is standing up. He (make) a speech.
18 He (grow) a beard when he leaves school.
19 This aeroplane (crash).
20 I (stop) here for a moment to get some petrol.
21 You (ask) him to help you?
22 I've lent you my car once. I (not do) it again.
23 I have seen the play. Now I (read) the book.
24 Small boy: I (be) a frogman when I grow up.
25 I (not sleep) in this room. It is haunted.
26 We (buy) a metal detector and look for buried treasure.
27 You (reserve) a seat?
28 I (plant) an oak tree here.
29 The dog (bury) the bone.
30 I (have) a bath.

Future forms

31 I (smuggle) this out of the country.
32 There was very little blossom this spring. Apples (be) scarce.
33 I don't like this macaroni. I (not finish) it.
34 I (not stay) here another minute.
35 They (try) him for manslaughter when he comes out of hospital.
36 We (make) a lot of money out of this.

47 The present continuous and the **be going to** form

◪ PEG 202–6

Planned future actions can be expressed by the present continuous
tense with a time expression or by the **be going to** form with or
without a time expression. The present continuous is mainly used
for very definite arrangements in the near future. The **be going to**
form can be used more widely.

Use the present continuous where possible in the following
sentences and put the remaining verbs into the **be going to** form.

1 I (play) bridge tonight with Tom and Ann.
2 He (have) an operation next week.
3 It's very cold. I (light) a fire.
4 We (have) some friends to lunch tomorrow.
5 I've bought a piano; it (be) delivered this afternoon. ~
Where you (put) it? ~
I (put) it in the dining room.
6 You (go) to the auction tomorrow? ~
Yes, I (go) but I (not buy) anything.
7 I've reminded you once; I (not do) it again.
8 I (have) my hair cut this afternoon.
9 My nephew (come) to stay with me next weekend. ~
Where you (put) him? ~
I (put) him in the room in the tower.
10 Our class (start) German next term.
11 I (spend) a few days in London next week.
12 The Town Council (build) a new school here.
13 What you (tell) the police? ~
I (tell) them the truth.
14 He (start) tomorrow.
15 The Queen (open) Parliament next month.
16 The Prime Minister (speak) on TV tonight.
17 This shop (close) down next week.
18 When you (have) your next lesson? ~
I (have) it on Monday.
19 I (collect) my new dress this afternoon.
20 We (take) the children to the seaside this summer.
21 I (give) him a football for his next birthday.

22 She (sing) in her first big concert next month.
23 He (go) to Spain for his holidays. ~
   He (fly)? ~
   No, he (go) by boat.
24 She (see) a specialist next week.
25 He (wash) the car?
26 He (ring) me up tonight.
27 The inspector (ask) you a few questions.
28 Her parents (give) a party for her next month. They (invite) sixty
   guests.
29 Have you got a ticket for the big match on Saturday? ~
   No, I don't even know who (play). ~
   France (play) England.
30 They (launch) a ship this afternoon. You (come) to see it?
31 What you (do) with the money?
32 I (pick) you up at 6.30; don't forget.
33 Where you (go) tonight? ~
   I (go) out with Peter. He (call) for me at eight.
34 I (compete) in the bicycle race tomorrow.
35 Mr Pitt has just phoned to say that he (not come) back till
   Wednesday night.
36 I (read) you his answer to my letter of complaint.

48 The future simple

☐ PEG 207-9

Put the verbs in brackets into the future simple.

1 I (know) the result in a week.
2 You (be) in Rome tonight.
3 You (have) time to help me tomorrow?
4 It (matter) if I don't come home till morning?
5 You (be) able to drive after another five lessons.
6 Do you think that he (recognize) me?
7 Unless he runs he (not catch) the train.
8 He (lend) it to you if you ask him.
9 I hope I (find) it.
10 If petrol pump attendants go on strike we (not have) any petrol.
11 He (believe) whatever you tell him.
12 I (remember) this day all my life.
13 Perhaps he (arrive) in time for lunch.
14 If he works well I (pay) him £10.
15 I wonder how many of us still (be) here next year.
16 If you think it over you (see) that I am right.
17 If you learn another language you (get) a better job.
18 I am sure that you (like) our new house.

19 Newspaper announcement: The President (drive) along the High Street in an open carriage.
20 He (mind) if I bring my dog?
21 You (need) a visa if you are going to Spain.
22 If you open that trapdoor you (see) some steps.
23 You (feel) better when you've had a meal.
24 He (be) offended if you don't invite him.
25 She (have) £1000 a year when she is twenty-one.
26 If you put any more polish on that floor someone (slip) on it.
27 I wonder if he (succeed).
28 Papers (not be) delivered on the Bank Holiday.
29 I hope he (remember) to buy wine.
30 If you leave your roller skates on the path someone (fall) over them.
31 If they fall over them and hurt themselves they (sue) you.
32 Announcement: Mrs Pitt (present) the prizes.
33 If you want twenty cigarettes you (have) to give me more money.
34 Notice: The management (not be) responsible for articles left on the seats.
35 If I drop this it (explode).
36 What your father (say) when he hears about this accident? ~
He (not say) much but he not (lend) me the car again.

49 The present continuous and the future simple

◢ PEG 202, 207-9

Put the verbs in brackets into the present continuous or the future simple using the present continuous where possible.

(The **be going to** form could be used here instead of the present continuous, but for the sake of simplicity students are advised to use only the two tenses first mentioned.)

1 I am sure that I (recognize) him.
2 I (see) her tomorrow.
3 He (play) in a tennis match on Friday.
4 She (come) back on Monday.
5 I (go) again next year.
6 We (know) tonight.
7 You pay and I (owe) you the money.
8 I (believe) it when I see it.
9 I (have) my car repainted next week.
10 I hope that you (have) a good time tomorrow.
11 His speech (be) broadcast tonight.
12 The window-cleaner (come) at eight tomorrow.
13 Tom (catch) the 7.40 train.
14 Where you (meet) them? ~
I (meet) them at midnight in the middle of the wood.

15 What horse you (ride) tomorrow?
16 Look! I've broken the teapot. What Mrs Pitt (say)? ~
    She (not mind); she never liked that one.
17 I've left the light on. It (matter)?
18 He (not forget) to come.
19 He (leave) in a few days.
20 I (remember) it.
21 If you drop that bottle it (break).
22 I never (forgive) him.
23 I'm sure that you (like) him.
24 They (lay) the foundations next week.
25 You (see) a signpost at the end of the road.
26 He has cut my hair too short. ~
    Don't worry; it (grow) again very quickly.
27 You (understand) when you are older.
28 The cat (scratch) you if you pull its tail.
29 I (be) back at 8.30.
30 If he doesn't work hard he (not pass) his exam.
31 She (go) on a cruise next summer.
32 I (move) to a new flat next week.
33 I am sorry that the child saw the accident. ~
    I don't think it matters. He soon (forget) all about it.
34 I (wait) here till he comes back.
35 He (not write) to you unless you write to him.
36 There (be) a big meeting here tomorrow.

50 will + infinitive and the be going to form

☑ PEG 201, 203–6

Future with intention can usually be expressed by **will** + infinitive
or the **be going to** form. Very often either of these can be used, but
when the intention is clearly premeditated the **be going to** form must
be used, and when the intention is clearly unpremeditated we must
use **will** + infinitive.

Put the verbs in brackets into one of these two forms. (In some of
the examples the present continuous could be used instead of the **be
going to** form.)

1 The fire has gone out! ~
   So it has. I (go) and get some sticks.
2 Did you remember to book seats? ~
   Oh no, I forgot. I (telephone) for them now.
3 He has just been taken to hospital with a broken leg. ~
   I'm sorry to hear that. I (send) him some grapes.
4 I've hired a typewriter and I (learn) to type.
5 I see that you have got a loom. You (do) some weaving?

Future forms

6 I can't understand this letter. ~
   I (call) my son. He (translate) it for you.
7 You (buy) meat? ~
   No, I (not eat) meat any more. I (eat) vegetables.
8 You've bought a lot of paint. You (redecorate) your kitchen?
9 Why are you getting out the jack? ~
   We have a puncture and I (change) the wheel. ~
   I (help) you.
10 Look what I've just bought at an auction! ~
   What an extraordinary thing! Where you (put) it?
11 Why are you peeling that bit of garlic? ~
   I (put) it in the stew.
12 What you (do) when you grow up? ~
   I (be) an acrobat in a circus.
13 What are you going to do with that dress? ~
   I (shorten) the skirt.
14 Will you lend me your season ticket? ~
   No, I (not lend) it to you. It is against the law.
15 That tree makes the house very dark. ~
   Very well, I (cut) it down.
16 I've just enrolled at the local technical college. I (attend) pottery
   classes next winter.
17 How do I get from here to London Bridge? ~
   I don't know, but I (ask) that policeman.
18 Why are you carrying a corkscrew? ~
   I (open) a bottle of wine.
19 Why's he putting the camera on a tripod? ~
   He (take) a group photo.
20 My brother has just returned from America. ~
   Oh good, we (ask) him to our next party.
21 Why have you set your alarm to go off at five-thirty? ~
   Because I (get) up then. I've got a lot to do.
22 I'm turning this cupboard into a darkroom. I (develop) my own films.
23 You look frozen. Sit down by the fire and I (make) you a cup of tea.
24 They've brought a rope and they (tow) the car to a garage.
25 I haven't bought any cigarettes because I (give) up smoking.
26 I have tried to explain but she doesn't understand English. ~
   I (say) it to her in Finnish: perhaps she'll understand that.
27 I've come out without any money. ~
   Never mind, I (lend) you some. How much do you want?
28 Do you see that car? They (raffle) it for charity.
29 They've hired a bulldozer. They (clear) away this rubble.
30 Child: I've torn my dress.
   Mother: I (mend) it for you.
31 I'm catching the 6.30 train. ~
   So am I. I (give) you a lift to the station.
32 I've bought some blue velvet and I (make) curtains for this room.

33 Why are you carrying that saw? ~
   I (shorten) the legs of the dining room table.
34 Why are you taking that big basket? ~
   I (buy) a lot of vegetables.
35 I've planned my future for the next ten years. ~
   That is very clever of you. What you (do) when you leave the
   university?
36 Why are you putting that old loaf into a paper bag? ~
   I (give) it to Mrs Pitt for her hens.

51 will + infinitive and the be going to form

☑ PEG 205

Both **will you** and **are you going to** can introduce questions about
future intentions. But **will you** very often introduces a request or
invitation. For this reason **are you going to** is more usual than **will
you** in questions about intentions. **are you going to** must of course be
used when the intention is obviously premeditated. (See also
Exercise 55.)

Put the verbs in brackets into one of these two forms. Where both
are possible it will be noted in the key. (In some examples the
present continuous tense could be used instead of the **be going to**
form.) The exercise contains requests, invitations, and questions
about intentions.

1 You (open) the door for me, please? ~
   Yes, certainly.
2 You (do) the washing-up tonight? ~
   No, I think it can wait till tomorrow.
3 I'm looking for my easel. ~
   You (paint) someone's portrait?
4 'You (read) this passage aloud, please,' said the examiner.
5 You (eat) any more of this, or shall I tell the waiter to take it away?
6 You aren't wearing your climbing boots. You (not climb) the
   mountain with the others?
7 'You (listen) to me!' said his mother angrily.
8 You (put) my car away from me, please? ~
   Yes, certainly.
9 You (have) another cup of coffee? ~
   No, thank you.
10 Why did you buy all these eggs? You (make) an enormous omelette?
11 There's the phone again. Take no notice. ~
   You (not answer) it?
12 You (come) and see me after the class? I want to discuss your work
   with you.
13 I see that you have ordered the *Guardian*. You really (read) it?

14 You (buy) stamps? ~
Yes, I am. ~
Then you (buy) some for me, please?
15 You (lend) me your fishing rod? ~
Yes, of course. Where you (fish)?
16 You (finish) this book or shall I take it back to the library?
17 You (give) me 10p, please? ~
Yes, here you are. You (make) a telephone call?
18 You (leave) that coil of barbed wire in the hall? Someone will fall
over it if you do.
19 You (bath) your dog? ~
Yes, you (help) me?
20 You (drive), please? I don't like driving at night.
21 You (ride) that horse? He looks very bad-tempered to me.
22 You (eat) it raw? You will be ill if you do.
23 You (have) some of this cake? I made it myself.
24 You really (call) the fire brigade? I don't think it is at all necessary.
25 You (paint) the whole room by yourself? It will take you ages.
26 You (be) ready in five minutes?
27 Hostess: John, you (sit) here at the end of the table?
28 You (do) something for me? ~
Yes, of course; what is it?
29 You (be) angry if he refuses to help you?
30 Why have you brought your typewriter? You (work) this weekend?
31 You (call) me at six? I have to catch an early train.
32 You (walk) there in this rain? You'll get awfully wet.
33 You (sign) here, please?
34 What are all those notes for? You (give) a lecture?
35 Why do you want a candle? You (explore) the caves?
36 If I catch some fish, you (cook) them for me?

52 The future continuous tense

☐ PEG 211–13

This tense can be used

1 with a point in time to indicate that the action will begin before
this time and continue after it.

2 with or without a time to express a future without intention. In
this way it is very like the present continuous, but it is not, like the
present continuous, restricted in time and is a more detached and
casual way of expressing the future. It often implies that the action
will occur in the ordinary course of events or as a matter of routine.

(Except when used as in 1, above, this tense can usually be replaced
by one of the other future forms, though the exact shade of meaning
may then be lost.)

Put the verbs in brackets into the future continuous tense.

1 This time next month I (sit) on a beach.
2 When you arrive I probably (pick) fruit.
3 When we reach England it very likely (rain).
4 In a few days time we (fly) over the Pyrenees.
5 I'll call for her at eight. ~
 No, don't; she still (have) breakfast then.
6 I (wait) for you when you come out.
7 When you next see me I (wear) my new dress.
8 My son will be in the sixth form next year. ~
 That means that old Dr Adder (teach) him mathematics.
9 I'll give Jack your message. I can do it easily because I (see) him tomorrow. We go to work on the same train.
10 You (do) geometry next term.
11 I'll look out for you at the parade. ~
 Do, but I (wear) uniform so you may find it hard to recognize me.
12 We have to do night duty here. I (do) mine next week.
13 In a hundred years' time people (go) to Mars for their holidays.
14 He (use) the car this afternoon.
15 I (see) you again.
16 It's a serious injury but he (walk) again in six weeks.
17 I'll come at three o'clock. ~
 Good, I (expect) you.
18 They are pulling down all the old houses in this street. I expect they (pull) down mine in a few years' time.
19 I'd like to see your new flat. ~
 Well, come tomorrow, but it (not look) its best, for the painters still (work) on it.
20 Stand there, they (change) the guard in a minute and you'll get a good view.
21 You'd better go back now; your mother (wonder) where you are.
22 In fifty years' time we (live) entirely on pills.
23 What do you think the children (do) when we get home? ~
 I expect they (have) their supper.
24 The garden (look) its best next month.
25 It won't be easy to get out of the country. The police (watch) all the ports.
26 What the tide (do) at six tomorrow morning? ~
 It (come) in.
27 I've just remembered that I left the bathroom taps on. I expect the water (flow) down the stairs by now.
28 You (need) your camera tomorrow or can I borrow it?
29 We've just got to the top in time. The sun (rise) in a minute.
30 Air hostess: We (take off) in a few minutes. Please fasten your safety belts.
31 We'd better go out tomorrow because Mary (practise) the piano all day.

Future forms

32 Don't ring her up at 6.00; she (put) the children to bed. Ring later.
33 We are making a house-to-house collection of things for the jumble sale. We (come) to your house next week.
34 That football club has lost some of its players. They (look out) for new men.
35 When I get home my dog (sit) at the door waiting for me.
36 Let's go down to the harbour; the fishing boats all (come) in because of the gale.

53 **will** + infinitive and the future continuous

☑ PEG 201, 211–14

See note for previous exercise.

Put the verbs in brackets into the appropriate future form, using **will** + infinitive or the future continuous. (Where alternative forms are possible they will be given in the key.)

1 There is going to be a bus strike. Everyone (walk) to work next week.
2 You've just missed the last train! ~
   Never mind, I (walk).
3 I'll ring you tomorrow at six. ~
   No, don't ring at six; I (bath) the baby then. Ring later.
4 Mother: Your face is dirty.
   Child: All right, I (wash) it.
5 Will you have lunch with me on the 24th? ~
   I'd love to, but I'm afraid I (do) my exam then.
6 I (work) for Mr Pitt next week as his own secretary will be away.
7 You (have) something to drink, won't you?
8 Why did you take his razor? He (look) for it everywhere tomorrow.
9 I hope you'll do well in the race tomorrow. I (think) of you.
10 Notice on board ship: In the event of an emergency all passengers (assemble) on the boat deck.
11 I don't feel well enough to go to the station to meet him. ~
   I (meet) him for you. But how I (recognize) him? ~
   He's small and fair, and he (wear) a black and white school cap.
12 I (leave) these flowers at the hospital for you. I (go) there anyway to visit my cousin.
13 You ought to try to get a ticket for the Spectators' Gallery next week; they (debate) international fishing rights.
14 You've left the light on. ~
   Oh, so I have. I (go) and turn it off.
15 I've just been appointed assistant at the local library. ~
   Then you (work) under my sister. She is head librarian there.

Error84

16 I want to post this letter but I don't want to go out in the rain. ~
   I (post) it for you. I (go) out anyway as I have to take the dog for a
   walk.
17 The prima ballerina is ill so I expect her understudy (dance) instead.
18 Today is Guy Fawkes' Day; this evening people (let) off fireworks
   and (make) bonfires in the streets.
19 Military order: Sentries (remain) on duty till they are relieved.
20 This time next Monday I (sit) in a Paris café reading *Le Figaro*. ~
   You (not read). You'll be looking at all the pretty girls.
21 Wages have gone up, so I suppose prices (go up) too.
22 It is nearly autumn; soon the leaves (change) colour.
23 Mother (on phone): My son has just burnt his hand very badly.
   Doctor: I (come) at once.
24 Customer in restaurant: Waiter, this plate is dirty.
   Waiter: I'm sorry, sir, I (bring) you another.
25 In a few years' time we all (live) in houses heated by solar energy.
26 It's beginning to get dark; the street lights (go on) in a few minutes.
27 We (not play) poker at the party tonight; our hostess doesn't approve
   of cards.
28 Let's wait here; the swing bridge (open) in a minute to let that ship
   through.
29 Guest: May I use your phone to ring for a taxi?
   Hostess: Oh, there's no need for that; my son (drive) you home.
30 Come on deck; we (enter) harbour in a few minutes.
31 Before you leave the office you (hand) the keys of the safe to Mr
   Pitt. Do you understand? ~
   Yes, sir.
32 Are you nearly ready? Our guests (arrive) any minute.
33 Loudspeaker announcement: The ship (leave) in a few minutes and
   all persons not travelling are asked to go ashore.
34 Now that the parking regulations have become stricter, more people
   (use) public transport and (leave) their cars at home.
35 I've got rats in my basement and I don't know how to get rid of
   them. ~
   I (bring) my dog round whenever you like. He (catch) them for you.
36 I'm afraid I've just broken your goldfish bowl. ~
   Never mind, I (put) the goldfish in the bath.

54 won't + infinitive and the future continuous negative
☑ PEG 214

won't + infinitive (except when used as part of the ordinary future
simple, **shall/will**) usually implies that the subject refuses to perform
a certain action. The negative future continuous tense merely states
that a certain action will not take place.

Future forms

Put the verbs in brackets into the appropriate future form, using
won't + infinitive or the future continuous negative. (Where other
future forms are also possible this will be noted in the key.)

1 I don't like that man and I (not help) him.
2 He (not meet) her, because they will be in different places.
3 My husband (not cut) down the tree. He says that it is perfectly all
   right as it is.
4 My husband (not cut) the hedge for some time, because he's got a lot
   of other jobs to do first.
5 Tom (not come) to our party, because he will be away on that date.
6 Peter says that he (not come) to our party. He doesn't approve of
   parties.
7 She says that she (not lend) me the book, because I never give books
   back.
8 Mr Pitt (not speak) at the meeting tonight, because he has
   unexpectedly had to go to hospital.
9 I'll work under anyone except my brother. I (not work) under him.
10 We'll be in the same firm, but we (not work) together, because we'll
    be in different departments.
11 I (not have) that boy in my class. He is far too noisy.
12 I (not teach) you next week, as I have to go to Paris.
13 He is so angry with his sister that he (not speak) to her.
14 I'll give your message to my sister when I write; but I (not write) for
    some time, as I only write once a month and I posted a letter to her
    yesterday.
15 I (not feed) your dog again. He always tries to bite me when I come
    near him.
16 They were very rude to me. I (not go) there again.
17 He said, 'I (not paint) you in that dress. It does not suit you.'
18 I (not take) any photographs for some time because my camera is
    being repaired.
19 I (not borrow) his van again. The brakes don't work properly.
20 That boy (not wash) his face. He likes being dirty.
21 You can have the car tomorrow if you like. I (not use) it as I'll be far
    too busy to go out.
22 She says that she (not send) the child to school, no matter what we
    say. She thinks it is far better to educate children at home.
23 He says he (not play) for them again, because they aren't giving him
    enough money.
24 She (not sing) at the next concert, because she has had to go home
    suddenly.
25 I (not play) cards with you again. You always cheat.
26 She (not take) part in the bridge tournament, because she'll be away
    then.
27 I (not eat) any more of this; I feel queer already.
28 I (not eat) curry again for a long time, because I am going to stay in
    a house where no one knows how to cook it.

29 He says that he (not ride) that mare again, because she's dangerous.
30 Tom (not ride) in tomorrow's race, because he is too young. They don't allow riders under sixteen.
31 Whisky is absolutely necessary to me and I (not give) it up.
32 Jack (not drink) whisky this time next week, because he'll be in hospital and they won't give it to him there.
33 I (not open) the window. I dislike fresh air.
34 There is something on his mind, but he (not tell) me what it is.
35 The cat (not eat) fish so I have to buy meat for him.
36 He (not wear) uniform when you see him, because he'll be on leave then, and they don't wear uniform when they are on leave.

55 Second person interrogative: **will you** and other forms
■ PEG 215 B

will you? often introduces a request or invitation, and sometimes a command. It is often used also to introduce questions about intentions when the situation requires an unpremeditated decision.
　　You can have either. Which will you have?
　　You've missed the last train. What will you do now?

For other types of intention, however, it is usually safer to use one of the other future forms: **be going to**, the present continuous or the future continuous (which is considered the most polite form).

Put the verbs in brackets into one of the four forms. When more than one answer is possible, this will be noted in the key.

1 Why are you taking all that bread with you? You (feed) the swans?
2 You (let) your flat again next summer?
3 You (light) the fire for me, please? Here are the matches.
4 You (wear) a tie tomorrow? ~
Oh no. Tom said, 'Come as you are.'
5 I know you don't like wearing ties, but (wear) one tomorrow, just to please me? ~
Yes, of course.
6 Shop assistant: You (come) this way, please?
7 You (have) something more to eat? ~
Yes, please, I'd like another sandwich.
8 You (have) anything more to eat? ~
No, because I haven't any more money.
9 You (study) computer programming at college?
10 You (speak) to Tom at the meeting tomorrow, do you think?
11 You (turn) off the TV, please? No one is watching it.
12 You (take) your exam now or in December?
13 You (listen) in to the concert this evening?
14 You (help) me with this, please? I can't lift it.

15 Hotel receptionist: You (stay) for more than one night, Mrs Jones?
16 You (lend) me your typewriter for an hour? I want to type a letter.
17 You (meet) him at the station? ~
   No, we never meet him. He doesn't like being met.
18 You (come) sailing with me this afternoon? ~
   No, thank you, I don't like sailing.
19 You (have) some more wine? ~
   Yes, please.
20 I can't understand this letter. You (translate) it for me, Miss Pitt?
21 You (use) your camera this afternoon? ~
   No, you can borrow it if you like.
22 You (go) to the tobacconist's? ~
   Yes. ~
   Then you (get) me twenty cigarettes?
23 You (come) to the Motor Show with me next Wednesday? ~
   Thank you very much. I'd love to.
24 I'll be going abroad next week. Is there anything I can get you? ~
   You (pass) through Paris? ~
   Yes, I (spend) a few days there. ~
   Then you (get) me some scent?
25 I see that you are repairing your old henhouse. You (keep) hens?
26 I've just bought my tickets. ~
   You (travel) by sea or air?
27 What are all these slates for? You (repair) your roof?
28 You (hold) my parcels, please, while I put up my umbrella?
29 You (go) to Madeira as usual this summer?
30 You kindly (explain) why you didn't do what I told you?
31 You (recognize) him, do you think?
32 I've chosen a school for my son. ~
   You (send) him to a public school or to a State school?
33 Passenger to bus conductor: You (tell) me where to get off, please?
34 You (go) by car? If so, would you give my brother a lift?
35 You (type) all night again? Because if so I think I'll go to a hotel.
36 You (stop) interrupting! I'll never get finished if you don't keep
   quiet.

56 shall and will

■ PEG 201, 207–8, 233–4

shall is correct for the first person of the future simple (except when
this form is used to express intention), but in the affirmative and
negative will is very often used instead, i.e. we can say, 'I/we will'
and 'I/we won't' instead of 'I/we shall' and 'I/we shan't'. In the
interrogative will should not be used to replace shall.

There are some rather old-fashioned or formal constructions where **shall** is used with the second or third persons. Here **shall** cannot be replaced by **will**. Such constructions are usually avoided but a few examples have been given below.

Use **will** or **shall** to fill the spaces in the following sentences. Sometimes either could be used.

1 When you are in bed I . . . be at work.
2 Who'll help me? ~
   I . . .
3 We will unite to resist oppression, and tyrants . . . not triumph over us. (*We won't let them triumph.*)
4 What . . . we do now? ~
   Wait.
5 You've been a good child, and when we get home you . . . have a sweet. (*I'll give you a sweet.*)
6 Your father . . . hear of this. (*I'll certainly tell him.*)
7 . . . we go to the cinema? ~
   Yes, let's.
8 She . . . tell the same story over and over again. (*obstinate insistence*)
9 Club rule: Members . . . write the names of their guests in the book provided.
10 Theatre regulation: Persons . . . not be permitted to sit in the gangways.
11 Where . . . I be in six years' time, I wonder?
12 He . . . not come here again. (*He refuses.*)
13 He . . . not come here again. (*I won't let him come.*)
14 Clause in lease: The tenant . . . be responsible for all repairs.
15 This kind of snake . . . not bite unless it is startled.
16 . . . you have a cigarette? ~
   No, thanks, I don't smoke.
17 He . . . play his radio very loudly, which annoys me very much. (*obstinate insistence*)
18 By this time next year I . . . be earning my own living.
19 Who . . . take this letter to the post for me? ~
   I . . .
20 What . . . we do with all the food that's left over?
21 Do you know the way? No? Then I . . . show you.
22 Where . . . I put it? ~
   Put it behind the piano.
23 Police notice: . . . anyone who witnessed the accident please ring 2222.
24 Yachts . . . go round the course, passing the marks in the correct order. (*extract from Yacht Racing Rules*)
25 When . . . you hear the result? ~
   I . . . not hear for another week.
26 'I . . . not apologize', she said, stamping her foot.

27 Who . . . I say called? ~
You needn't mention my name. He . . . know who I am.
28 She . . . never do anything you tell her.
29 I . . . not be here next week.
30 I . . . not have to do any cooking for a month. I'm going to an hotel.
31 . . . I put it on your desk? ~
Please do.
32 I . . . fill up this form! The questions are impertinent. ~
If you don't, madam, you . . . (*negative*) get your visa.
33 . . . you stand quite still for a moment, please?
34 . . . I put more salt in the stew?
35 A dog . . . obey his owner but a cat . . . not.
36 I . . . know whether you are telling the truth or not.

57 Time clauses

☐ PEG 342

The future simple is not used in time clauses, the simple present tense being used instead.

Put the verbs in brackets into the correct tense (present or future).

1 When he (return) I'll give him the key.
2 He'll be ready as soon as you (be).
3 I'll stay in bed till the clock (strike) seven.
4 She will be delighted when she (hear) this.
5 When the laundry comes I (have) some clean handkerchiefs.
6 I shan't buy tomatoes till the price (come) down.
7 Stay here till the lights (turn) green.
8 When it (get) cold I'll light the fire.
9 The lift (not start) until you press that button.
10 She'll have to behave better when she (go) to school.
11 When you look at yourself in the glass you (see) what I mean.
12 He (be) here before you go.
13 I (lend) you my cassette recorder whenever you want it.
14 He (wake) up when we turn the lights on.
15 He (ring) us up when he arrives in England?
16 He will wash up before he (go) to bed.
17 I won't come to London till the bus strike (be) over.
18 I (give) the childen their dinner before he (come) home.
19 They will be astonished when they (see) how slowly he works.
20 I'll pay you when I (get) my cheque.
21 I (go) on doing it until he tells me to stop.
22 I'll buy that house when I (have) enough money.
23 You (fall) rapidly through the air till your parachute opens.
24 We'll have to stay here till the tide (go) out.
25 When the Queen (arrive) the audience will stand up.

26 When the fog (lift) we'll be able to see where we are.
27 The refrigerator (go on) making that noise till we have it repaired.
28 As soon as the holidays begin this beach (become) very crowded.
29 The car (not move) till you take the brake off.
30 The alarm bell (go on) ringing till you press this button.
31 As soon as she (learn) to type I'll get her a job.
32 Look before you (leap). (*proverb*)
33 We (have) to stay on this desert island till we can repair our boat.
34 Don't count on a salary increase before you actually (get) it.
35 When winter (begin) the swallows will fly away to a warmer country.
36 We can't make any decision till he (arrive) here.

58 The future perfect tense

☐ PEG 216

Put the verbs in brackets into the future perfect tense.

1 In a fortnight's time we (take) our exam.
2 I (finish) this book by tomorrow evening.
3 By this time tomorrow we (have) our injections.
4 By the end of next year I (be) here twenty-five years.
5 I'll still be here next summer but Tom (leave).
6 I (finish) this job in twenty minutes.
7 By next winter they (build) four houses in that field.
8 When we reach Valparaiso we (sail) all round the world.
9 At the rate he is going he (spend) all his money by the time he is twenty-one.
10 By this time next year I (save) £250.
11 By the time we get to the party everything (be) eaten.
12 The train (leave) before we reach the station.
13 If I continue with my diet I (lose) 10 kilos by the end of the month.
14 By the end of my university course I (attend) 1,200 lectures.
15 By the end of this week my illness (cost) me £100.
16 By the time that he leaves school his parents (spend) £25,000 on his education.
17 By the end of the term I (read) all twelve volumes.
18 When you come back I (finish) all the housework.
19 The police (hear) of the theft by this time.
20 We (drink) all that wine by the end of the year.
21 On the fourth of next month he (be) in prison for ten years.
22 When we reach Crewe we (do) half of the journey.
23 At this rate you (break) all the wine glasses by the end of the month.
24 If we don't hurry the sun (rise) before we reach the top.
25 I'm going to Hyde Park to hear the people making speeches. ~
You'll be too late. By the time you get there they (finish) their speeches and everybody (go) home.

26 By midnight he (be) unconscious for forty-eight hours.
27 By the end of the month 5,000 people (see) this exhibition.
28 By next April I (pay) £3,000 in income tax.
29 I suppose that when I come back in ten years' time all these old houses (be) pulled down.
30 On 21 October they (be) married for twenty-five years.
31 After this performance I (see) *Hamlet* twenty-two times.
32 The strike leader said, 'By midnight 500 men (come) out on strike.'
33 At your present rate you (burn) all that coal by the end of the month.
34 The treasurer said, 'By the end of the year all our debts (be paid) off.'
35 Tourist: We've only got five hours in Rome; we are leaving at six; but I'm sure that we (see) everything of importance by then.
36 Householder to Zoo: One of your elephants is in my garden eating my tomatoes.
    Zoo official: The elephant keeper will be with you in half an hour.
    Householder: Your elephant (eat) all my tomatoes by then.

59 Time clauses

◪ PEG 342

The future perfect tense is not used in time clauses, the present perfect being used instead.

Put the verbs in brackets into the correct tense, using the future, present, or present perfect. Compare 1 to 5 with 1 to 5 in Exercise 58.

1 When we (take) our exam we'll have a holiday.
2 When I (finish) the book I'll lend it to you.
3 When we (have) our injections I expect we'll feel awful.
4 When I (be) here for a year I'll ask for a rise.
5 When Tom (go) I'll tell you a secret.
6 By the time he (get) back from his holiday the milkman will have left twenty-one bottles of milk outside his door.
7 Don't drive at more than 50 k.p.h. till your car (do) 4,000 kilometres.
8 When you (do) 4,000 kilometres you can drive it at 70 k.p.h.
9 When you open the safe you (see) a small black box.
10 When we (have) lunch we'll go for a walk.
11 When the bell rings I (take) the meat out of the oven.
12 I'll bolt all the doors before I (go) to bed.
13 When we (see) the cathedral we'll go to the museum.
14 We'll have to stay up this tree till the bull (go) away.
15 He (not let) you out till you have finished your homework.
16 As soon as I hear from him I (let) you know.
17 My father will be furious when he (see) what you have done.

18 You (not hear) the sound of the explosion till after you have seen the flash.
19 These gates will remain shut until the train (pass).
20 When he (sell) all his newspapers he'll go home.
21 We can't have a fire here until we (sweep) the chimney.
22 You (get) a shock when you open that box.
23 When you are eighteen your father (give) you a latchkey.
24 Don't jump out of the aeroplane until the pilot (say) 'Go!'
25 I can't leave the country till the police (return) my passport.
26 When a bottle of champagne (be) opened for twenty-four hours the wine is not fit to drink.
27 Hotel receptionist: When you (sign) the hotel register the porter will show you your room.
28 You (not know) how good oysters are till you have tasted one.
29 That road will not be safe till the floods (subside).
30 When everybody (leave) the park the park-keeper will lock the gates.
31 When we have seen the Chamber of Horrors we (have) a cup of tea.
32 When you (have) something to eat you'll feel better.
33 I (stay) in court till the jury returns.
34 You cannot become a member of this club until you (make) a parachute descent.
35 When the boa constrictor (eat) the goat he will become very lethargic.
36 As soon as everybody has gone to bed the mice (come) out of their holes.

60 would and should

■ PEG 140–1, 230–2, 235–7

Put **should** or **would** in the spaces in the following sentences.

1 . . . you mind opening the door?
2 . . . you like another cup of coffee?
3 He insisted that the newspaper . . . print an apology.
4 The old admiral . . . sit for hours watching the ships.
5 . . . you be so good as to keep an eye on my house while I am away?
6 I . . . say nothing about it if I were you.
7 That dress doesn't suit you; you . . . buy another.
8 If you pulled the communication cord the train . . . stop and you . . . be fined.
9 They went to the cinema at 2.30, so they . . . be back here by 6.00.
10 . . . you please help me with this?
11 It is very strange that he . . . think that.
12 I wish he . . . not play his radio so loudly.
13 . . . you be very kind and lend me your typewriter?

14 I . . . like to know where you have been.
15 It was decided that the matter . . . be referred to a special committee.
16 Perhaps you . . . be kind enough to let us know about this.
17 If the telephone . . . ring please say that I'll be back at six.
18 . . . you like to come or . . . you rather stay here?
19 There are too many accidents. Everyone . . . be much more careful.
20 Their method was always the same; they . . . wait till their victim had left the bank and then go up to him and ask for a light.
21 What are you doing here? You . . . be in bed.
22 It is essential that this matter . . . be kept out of the newspapers.
23 He suggested that the money . . . be raised by public subscription.
24 If you . . . change your mind, this address will always find me.
25 If this machine . . . at any time fail to give complete satisfaction please post us the enclosed card.
26 He changed his name so that nobody . . . know what he had been before.
27 If he offered me money I . . . refuse.
28 I wish you . . . not ask so many questions.
29 He ordered that Tom . . . leave the house at once.
30 I . . . be most grateful if you . . . do this for me.
31 He is anxious that everyone . . . understand why he acted as he did.
32 You . . . not argue with your father; you . . . obey him.
33 He was a very patient cat; he . . . sit for hours beside a mousehole.
34 . . . the pain return take one of these pills.
35 It is most important that I . . . see him at once.
36 He didn't dare (to) sell the ring in case someone . . . ask where he got it.

61 **would** and **should**

■ PEG 140–1, 230–2, 235–7

Put **should** or **would** in the spaces in the following sentences:

1 It is only fair that you . . . know the truth about your own father and it is better that you . . . hear it from me than from some stranger.
2 If you . . . kindly wait here a moment I'll ring the director's office.
3 . . . these measures fail to restore order harsher restrictions will have to be imposed.
4 The rocks were icy and he was terrified lest he . . . slip.
5 If Pierre liked any dish he . . . send for the chef and congratulate him, and if anything was wrong he . . . send for the manager and complain. ~
An Englishman . . . never dare to do that; he . . . be too shy.
6 I was just burying the bones in the garden when who . . . look over the hedge but the village policeman.

7 When he found out that the man had smallpox he urged that every effort . . . be made to contact his fellow passengers.

8 I wish you . . . go out or sit down. How . . . you like it if I kept tramping round when you were trying to work?

9 I've just received an anonymous threatening letter. What . . . I do about it? ~
I . . . take it to the police if I were you.

10 The committee thinks that you have been guilty of disloyalty. ~
I don't know why the committee . . . think that.

11 I can't repair it now but if you . . . like to leave it with me I'll see what can be done.

12 You complained to the manager, of course? ~
No, I asked to speak to him but he . . . not come to the phone. ~
You . . . have insisted.

13 Where will he be now? ~
Oh, he . . . be there by now; the flight only takes an hour.

14 If your main parachute . . . fail to open, your second one will open automatically.

15 I suggested that Tom . . . walk on and try to get help while I stayed with the injured man but he . . . not hear of this.

16 I am amazed that you . . . even suggest offering bribes.

17 This passage doesn't lead anywhere. It is odd that no one . . . have noticed this before.

18 . . . you mind not smoking; this is the petrol store. ~
Then there . . . be a 'No Smoking' notice.

19 Can't I trust you not to read my letters? It is ridiculous that I . . . have to lock things up in my own house.

20 He said he wished I . . . not come so often.

21 This train is entirely automatic; there is no driver; but a mechanic is always available in case anything . . . go wrong.

22 She had one rather boring habit; she . . . insist on telling people about her dreams.

23 He recommended that the trouble makers in the factory . . . be dismissed.

24 It is absurd that women . . . be paid less than men for doing the same work.

25 I . . . rather you asked him. Last time I tried to speak to him he . . . not listen.

26 When he went out he left the radio on so that his parents . . . think that he was still in his room.

27 He was determined that his children . . . go to the best schools available.

28 Tom says you are foolish to take such a risk. ~
He . . .! (*That is typical of him.*)

29 When four hours had passed and there was still no sign of him she began to be worried lest he . . . have met with some accident.

30 People are very fond of saying, 'This . . . be stopped', or,
'Something . . . be done about this', but if they were the government
they . . . not know how to stop it or what to do about it.

31 It is amazing that the Leaning Tower of Pisa . . . have stood for so
long.

32 He resigned from the government in order that everyone . . . know
that he disapproved of the new policy.

33 If I had had his education and he had had mine perhaps I . . . be
sitting at his desk and he . . . be out here sweeping the streets.

34 He was a terribly obstinate child, who . . . never obey the simplest
order, but . . . argue every point till she nearly went mad.

35 Robinson said, 'Why . . . Smith get all the credit when someone else
has done all the work?'

36 All day he . . . sit in his office immaculately dressed, but at night he
. . . put on dirty ragged clothing and roam about the streets with
disreputable companions.

5 Conditionals

62 Conditional sentences: type 1

◢ PEG 221

Put the verbs in brackets into the correct tenses.

1 If I see him I (give) him a lift.
2 The table will collapse if you (stand) on it.
3 If he (eat) all that he will be ill.
4 If I find your passport I (telephone) you at once.
5 The police (arrest) him if they catch him.
6 If he (read) in bad light he will ruin his eyes.
7 Someone (steal) your car if you leave it unlocked.
8 What will happen if my parachute (not open)?
9 If he (wash) my car I'll give him £10.
10 If she (need) a radio she can borrow mine.
11 If you (not go) away I'll send for the police.
12 I'll be very angry if he (make) any more mistakes.
13 If he (be) late we'll go without him.
14 She will be absolutely furious if she (hear) about this.
15 If you put on the kettle I (make) the tea.
16 If you give my dog a bone he (bury) it at once.
17 If we leave the car here it (not be) in anybody's way.
18 He'll be late for the train if he (not start) at once.
19 If you come late they (not let) you in.
20 If he (go) on telling lies nobody will believe a word he says.
21 Unless he (sell) more he won't get much commission.
22 If I lend you £10 when you (repay) me?
23 We'll have to move upstairs if the river (rise) any higher.
24 If he (work) hard today can he have a holiday tomorrow?
25 Ice (turn) to water if you heat it.
26 If the house (burn) down we can claim compensation.
27 If you (not like) this one I'll bring you another.
28 Unless you are more careful you (have) an accident.
29 Tell him to ring me up if you (see) him.
30 If I tell you a secret, you (promise) not to tell it to anyone else?
31 If you (not believe) what I say, ask your mother.
32 If he (like) the house will he buy it?
33 If you will kindly sit down I (make) enquiries for you.
34 Unless I have a quiet room I (not be able) to do any work.
35 She won't open the door unless she (know) who it is.
36 Should you require anything else please (ring) the bell for the attendant.

63 Conditional sentences: type 2

☑ PEG 222

Put the verbs in brackets into the correct tenses.

1 If I had a typewriter I (type) it myself.
2 If I (know) his address I'd give it to you.
3 He (look) a lot better if he shaved more often.
4 If you (play) for lower stakes you wouldn't lose so much.
5 If he worked more slowly he (not make) so many mistakes.
6 I shouldn't drink that wine if I (be) you.
7 More tourists would come to this country if it (have) a better climate.
8 If I were sent to prison you (visit) me?
9 If someone (give) you a helicopter what would you do with it?
10 I (buy) shares in that company if I had some money.
11 If he (clean) his windscreen he'd be able to see where he was going.
12 If you drove your car into the river you (be able) to get out?
13 If you (not belong) to a union you couldn't get a job.
14 If I (win) a big prize in a lottery I'd give up my job.
15 What you (do) if you found a burglar in your house?
16 I could tell you what this means if I (know) Greek.
17 If everybody (give) £1 we would have enough.
18 He might get fat if he (stop) smoking.
19 If he knew that it was dangerous he (not come).
20 If you (see) someone drowning what would you do?
21 I (be) ruined if I bought her everything she asked for.
22 If you slept under a mosquito net you (not be) bitten so often.
23 I could get a job easily if I (have) a degree.
24 If she (do) her hair differently she might look quite nice.
25 If we had more rain our crops (grow) faster.
26 The whole machine would fall to pieces if you (remove) that screw.
27 I (keep) a horse if I could afford it.
28 I'd go and see him more often if he (live) on a bus route.
29 If they (ban) the sale of alcohol at football matches there might be less violence.
30 I (offer) to help if I thought I'd be any use.
31 What would you do if the lift (get) stuck between two floors?
32 If you (paint) the walls white the room would be much brighter.
33 If you (change) your job would it affect your pension?
34 If you knew you had only six weeks to live how you (spend) those six weeks?
35 You wouldn't have so much trouble with your car if you (have) it serviced regularly.
36 I'd climb over the wall if there (not be) so much broken glass on top of it.

64 Conditional sentences: type 3

☑ PEG 223

Put the verbs in brackets into the correct tenses.

1 If I had known that you were in hospital I (visit) you.
2 The ground was very soft. But for that, my horse (win).
3 If you (arrive) ten minutes earlier you would have got a seat.
4 You would have seen my garden at its best if you (be) here last week.
5 But for his quickness I (be) killed.
6 I shouldn't have believed it if I (not see) it with my own eyes.
7 If he had slipped he (fall) 500 metres.
8 If he had asked you, you (accept)?
9 If I (had) a map I would have been all right.
10 If I (know) that you were coming I'd have baked a cake.
11 I (offer) to help him if I had realized that he was ill.
12 If you had left that wasp alone it (not sting) you.
13 If I (realize) what a bad driver you were I wouldn't have come with you.
14 If I had realized that the traffic lights were red I (stop).
15 But for the fog we (reach) our destination ages ago.
16 If you had told me that he never paid his debts I (not lend) him the money.
17 If you (not sneeze) he wouldn't have known that we were there.
18 If you (put) some mustard in the sandwiches they would have tasted better.
19 The hens (not get) into the house if you had shut the door.
20 If he had known that the river was dangerous he (not try) to swim across it.
21 If you (speak) more slowly he might have understood you.
22 If he had known the whole story he (not be) so angry.
23 I shouldn't have eaten it if I (know) that there was ginger in it.
24 If I (try) again I think that I would have succeeded.
25 You (not get) into trouble if you had obeyed my instructions.
26 If you hadn't been in such a hurry you (not put) sugar into the sauce instead of salt.
27 If I (be) ready when he called he would have taken me with him.
28 She had a headache; otherwise she (come) with us.
29 If she had listened to my directions she (not turn) down the wrong street.
30 If you (look) at the engine for a moment you would have seen what was missing.
31 Rome (be captured) by her enemies if the geese hadn't cackled.
32 He would have been arrested if he (try) to leave the country.
33 I (take) a taxi if I had realized that it was such a long way.
34 You (save) me a lot of trouble if you had told me where you were going.

Conditionals

35 They would have forced their way into the house if I (not call) for help.
36 If he had put out his pipe before putting it in his pocket he (not burn) a hole in his coat.

65 Conditional sentences: mixed types

■ PEG 221–6

Put the verbs in brackets into the correct tenses.

1 If you (find) a skeleton in the cellar don't mention it to anyone.
2 If you pass your examination we (have) a celebration.
3 What (happen) if I press this button?
4 I should have voted for her if I (have) a vote then.
5 If you go to Paris where you (stay)?
6 If someone offered to buy you one of those rings, which you (choose)?
7 The flight may be cancelled if the fog (get) thick.
8 If the milkman (come) tell him to leave two pints.
9 Someone (sit) on your glasses if you leave them there.
10 You would play better bridge if you (not talk) so much.
11 What I (do) if I hear the burglar alarm?
12 If you (read) the instructions carefully you wouldn't have answered the wrong question.
13 I could repair the roof myself if I (have) a long ladder.
14 Unless they turn that radio off I (go) mad.
15 If you were made redundant what you (do)?
16 We'll have a long way to walk if we (run) out of petrol here.
17 If you shake that bottle of port it (not be) fit to drink.
18 I'll probably get lost unless he (come) with me.
19 You (not have) so many accidents if you drove more slowly.
20 If you (wear) a false beard nobody would have recognized you.
21 If she (leave) the fish there the car will get it.
22 Unless they leave a lamp beside that hole in the road somebody (fall) into it.
23 You'll get pneumonia if you (not change) your wet clothes.
24 If I had known that you couldn't eat octopus I (not buy) it.
25 If they (hang) that picture lower people would be able to see it.
26 She (be able) to walk faster if her shoes hadn't such high heels.
27 I (bring) you some beer if I had known that you were thirsty.
28 If you had touched that electric cable you (be) electrocuted.
29 If the story hadn't been true the newspaper (not print) it.
30 I (not buy) things on the instalment system if I were you.
31 Dial 999 if you (want) Police, Ambulance, or Fire Brigade.
32 You (not be) any use to me unless you learn to type.
33 If anyone attacked me, my dog (jump) at his throat.

34 If he were in he (answer) the phone.
35 The ship would have run aground if the pilot (make) one mistake.
36 I shouldn't have taken your umbrella if I (know) that it was the only one you had.

66 Conditional sentences: mixed types

■ PEG 221-6

Finish these sentences, taking care to use the correct tenses.

1 If he had taken my advice . . .
2 If you ate less . . .
3 We'll send for the doctor if . . .
4 If she practised more . . .
5 If there isn't enough wine in that bottle . . .
6 If you had checked the petrol before we started . . .
7 This clock wouldn't have run down if . . .
8 Try on the blue one if . . .
9 If these gates are locked . . .
10 If we leave before breakfast . . .
11 If the river rises any higher . . .
12 Her life might have been saved if . . .
13 If the volcano starts erupting . . .
14 The grass would look better if . . .
15 Unless it is a nice day . . .
16 If you don't put enough stamps on a letter, the person who gets it . . .
17 He would lend it to you if . . .
18 Unless this hotel gets another cook . . .
19 If the storm becomes worse . . .
20 If your uncle sees you . . .
21 If you tried to climb it without a guide . . .
22 If you didn't shake the camera so much, your photographs . . .
23 I'd have brought my coat . . .
24 If (=as) you don't like the picture . . .
25 He would have given her diamonds if . . .
26 If you had asked his permission . . .
27 If the fire had been noticed earlier . . .
28 If you had any sense . . .
29 You would have been angry if . . .
30 If he had put the flowers into water at once . . .
31 I should have ordered more coal if . . .
32 If you leave the gate open . . .
33 You will have to go to the dentist if . . .
34 He would have been drowned if . . .
35 If I'd had a car . . .
36 If Tom rings while I'm out . . .

67 Mixed tenses and verb forms

■ PEG 221–6, 283–4

Conditional forms are used in requests.
Fill the gaps in the following dialogue with a suitable verb form.

Telephone conversation

1 Ann: . . . I . . . to Mr Wash, please?
2 Wash: Wash . . .
3 Ann: Good morning, Mr Wash. This is Ann Jones of 10 Cyprus Road.
 . . . you come and . . . my windows one Saturday this month?
4 Wash: I'm afraid I . . . (*negative*). The next six Saturdays are already booked.
5 But I . . . . . . on Wednesday morning.
6 Ann: . . . you . . . very early on Wednesday? I leave at 8.15 on weekdays.
7 Wash: I . . . . . . to you by 8.30. . . . that be early enough?
8 Ann: No, it . . .! There . . . be nobody to let you in.
 I . . . the flat at 8.15.
9 Wash: Oh 8.15! I . . . you . . . 8.30!
10 Well, I suppose I . . . . . . to you by 8.00 as you're an old customer.
 But I . . . (*negative*) . . . a habit of it.
11 It means . . . breakfast at 6 and my wife . . . (*negative*) that.
12 She . . . always . . . to persuade me to give up window— . . . as it is.
 She . . . it's dangerous.
13 Ann: What . . . she . . . you . . . instead?
14 Wash: Her father has a shop and she . . . . . . me . . . . . . in it.
15 She . . . it . . . be a nice steady job with regular hours.
16 And if I . . . in a shop she . . . . . . where I was.
17 Ann: And . . . you really . . . of giving it up?
18 Wash: No, I . . . the life. At least, I . . . it in summer.
19 Besides, I . . . . . . bored working in a shop.
20 Well, . . . Wednesday at 8.00 . . . you then, Miss Jones?
21 Ann: Yes, it . . . be splendid. It's very good of you . . . . . . so early.
22 I . . . let you in and you can . . . yourself out.
23 You . . . shut the door carefully after you, . . . (*negative interrogative*) you?
24 Wash: Yes, of course I . . . . I always . . . . Goodbye, Miss Jones.

6 Infinitive

68 Full or bare infinitive

◪ PEG 246

Insert **to** where necessary before the infinitives in brackets.

1 He made me (do) it all over again.
2 She can (sing) quite well.
3 He will be able (swim) very soon.
4 I used (live) in a caravan.
5 You ought (go) today. It may (rain) tomorrow.
6 You needn't (say) anything. Just nod your head and he will (understand).
7 I want (see) the house where our president was born.
8 He made her (repeat) the message.
9 May I (use) your phone?
10 You needn't (ask) for permission; you can (use) it whenever you like.
11 If you want (get) there before dark you should (start) at once.
12 I couldn't (remember) his address.
13 You'll be able (do) it yourself when you are older.
14 Would you like (go) now or shall we (wait) till the end?
15 They won't let us (leave) the Customs shed till our luggage has been examined.
16 How dare you (open) my letters!
17 He didn't dare (argue) with his boss.
18 I used (smoke) forty cigarettes a day.
19 Will you help me (move) the bookcase?
20 He wouldn't let my baby (play) with his gold watch.
21 They refused (accept) the bribe.
22 He is expected (arrive) in a few days.
23 Please let me (know) your decision as soon as possible.
24 He made us (wait) for hours.
25 Could you (tell) me the time, please?
26 We must (send) him a telegram.
27 I let him (go) early as he wanted (meet) his wife.
28 Where would you like (have) lunch?
29 You can (leave) your dog with us if you don't (want) (take) him with you.
30 I'd like him (go) to a university but I can't (make) him (go).
31 We could (go) to a concert, unless you'd prefer (visit) a museum.
32 You seem (know) this area very well. ~
    Yes, I used (live) here.

Infinitive

33 The kidnappers told the parents (not inform) the police, and the parents didn't dare (disobey).
34 Need I (come)? I'd much rather (stay) at home.
35 You can (take) a horse to water but you can't (make) him (drink). (*proverb*)
36 I'm sorry (disappoint) you but I can't (let) you (have) any more money till the end of the month.

69 Full or bare infinitive

◪ PEG 246

Insert **to** where necessary before the infinitives in brackets. (In some of the sentences a present participle could be used instead of an infinitive. These alternatives will be noted in the key.)

1 It is easy (be) wise after the event.
2 Do you (wish) (make) a complaint?
3 We don't (want) anybody (know) that we are here.
4 If you can't (remember) his number you'd better (look) it up.
5 I want her (learn) Esperanto; I think everybody ought to (know) it.
6 He is said (be) the best surgeon in the country.
7 Visitors are asked (not feed) the animals.
8 Could I (see) Mr Pitt, please? ~
I'm afraid Mr Pitt isn't in. Would you like (speak) to his secretary?
9 It's better (travel) hopefully than (arrive). (*proverb*)
10 He should (know) how (use) the film projector, but if he doesn't you had better (show) him.
11 He was made (sign) a paper admitting his guilt.
12 I heard the door (open) and saw a shadow (move) across the floor.
13 He tried (make) me (believe) that he was my stepbrother.
14 As we seem (have missed) the train we may as well (go) back to the house.
15 I felt the house (shake) with the explosion.
16 He told me (try) (come) early.
17 Before he let us (go) he made us (promise) (not tell) anyone what we had seen.
18 Would you (like) (come) in my car? ~
No, thanks, I'd rather (walk).
19 I advised him (ask) the bus conductor (tell) him where (get) off.
20 It is better (put) your money in a bank than (keep) it under your bed in an old stocking.
21 He doesn't even bother (read) letters, let alone (answer) them.
22 The bank robbers made the cashier (show) them how (open) the safe
23 If you knew he was wrong, why didn't you (say) something? ~
I didn't like (say) anything because he always gets angry if you contradict him.

24 It's better (be) sure than sorry.
25 What do you (want) me (tell) him? ~
   Tell him that any time he cares (call) I shall be delighted (discuss)
   the matter with him.
26 Did you remember (give) him the money? ~
   No, I didn't, I still have it in my pocket; but I'll (see) him tonight and
   I promise (not forget) this time.
27 I saw the driver (open) his window and (throw) a box into the
   bushes.
28 That is far too heavy for one person (carry); let me (help) you.
29 I was afraid (pick) up the revolver as I don't know how (handle)
   firearms.
30 I saw the plane (crash) into the hill and (burst) into flames.
31 There is nothing (do) but (wait) till somebody comes (let) us out.
32 He heard a cock (crow) in a neighbouring village.
33 You may as well (tell) us the truth. It will (be) easy (check) your
   story.
34 The American said he had seen nine presidents (come) and (go). ~
   He must (be) a very old man.
35 It is up to you (learn) the laws of your own country.
36 Would you rather (be) more stupid than you look or (look) more
   stupid than you are?

70 Infinitive represented by **to**

☑ PEG 247

In each of the following pairs of sentences an infinitive used in the
first sentence is repeated in the second. Read the sentences,
expressing this second infinitive by **to** only. Note that where the
second infinitive has an object, this word/phrase must be omitted.
   Why didn't you tell me the truth the first time? ~
   I meant to tell you the truth but I was too frightened.
   I meant to but I was too frightened.

1 Did you visit the Pyramids? ~
   No, I wanted to visit them but there wasn't time.
2 Why do you wear dark glasses? ~
   I have to wear them; I have weak eyes.
3 Do you smoke? ~
   No, I used to smoke but I don't now.
4 Would you like to go to the theatre tonight? ~
   Yes, I'd love to go to the theatre.
5 Why didn't you pay the bill for him? ~
   I offered to pay it but he refused.
6 Have you put the car in the garage? ~
   No, but I'm just going to put it there.

Infinitive

7 I want you two to apologize to each other. ~
   Well, I am willing to apologize if he apologizes first.
8 Did you reserve seats on the train? ~
   No, I tried to reserve them but they had all been booked already.
9 Did you answer the letter? ~
   No, I intended to answer it but I'm afraid I forgot
10 Why didn't you hit him? ~
   I was afraid to hit him.
11 I'd love to spend a night in a haunted room. ~
   I'd hate to spend a night in a haunted room.
12 Why didn't you ask your father for the money? ~
   I didn't like to ask him.
13 Did you get a chance to fly the aeroplane yourself? ~
   No, I wanted to fly it but the pilot wouldn't let me.
14 Why doesn't he punish his boys when they disobey him? ~
   He often threatens to punish them but he never actually does so.
15 Why didn't he repair the car himself? ~
   He wasn't able to repair it.
16 I used to drink whisky with my meals. ~
   I used to drink whisky with my meals also but I don't now.
17 Did you buy sausages? ~
   No, I meant to buy them but I forgot.
18 Why doesn't he try again? ~
   He doesn't want to try again.
19 You should visit the Prado when you are in Madrid. ~
   Yes, I intend to visit it.
20 Why doesn't he play games? ~
   His mother doesn't want him to play games.
21 You ought to stop work now. ~
   Yes, I am just going to stop.
22 Why do some jockeys carry extra weights? ~
   They are obliged to carry them by the regulations.
23 Did he help you? ~
   No, I asked him to help me but he said he hadn't time.
24 You should have thanked her before you left. ~
   I meant to thank her but when I was going I couldn't find her anywhere.
25 Why did she put parsley in the soup? ~
   I told her to put it in.
26 Why didn't he report it to the police? ~
   He was afraid to report it. He didn't think they'd believe him.
27 Why did he drive so fast? ~
   He had to drive fast; otherwise he'd have missed his train.
28 You used to like rice pudding. ~
   Yes, I know I used to like it but I don't now.
29 Why didn't you buy the car? ~
   I was advised not to buy it.

30 I hope the children won't go near the water. ~
   I warned them not to go near it.
31 Why are we trying to get planning permission? ~
   We have to get planning permission. It is the law.
32 I meant to work hard. ~
   I know you meant to work hard but you didn't.
33 Do the boys tidy their own rooms? ~
   They are supposed to tidy them but they don't always.
34 Why didn't he call the police. ~
   He wasn't able to call them. His telephone line had been cut.
35 Why did you move your car? ~
   The policeman told me to move it.
36 Why did you bring your mother-in-law? I particularly asked you not to bring her.

71 too/enough/so . . . as with infinitive

☐ PEG 252

Combine each of the following pairs of sentences into one sentence using **too/enough** with infinitive.
   It is very cold. We can't go out.
   It is too cold for us to go out.
   He is strong. He can carry it.
   He is strong enough to carry it.

Rewrite numbers 3, 20, and 35 using **so . . . as** with infinitive.
(**enough** with infinitive could also be used here, while **so . . . as** could replace **enough** in numbers 9, 24, and 29. These alternatives are given in the key.)

1 You are very young. You can't have a front-door key.
2 It is very cold. We can't bathe.
3 Would you be very kind and answer this letter by return?
4 I am rather old. I can't wear that kind of hat.
5 The ladder wasn't very long. It didn't reach the window.
6 He hadn't much money. He couldn't live on it. (*Omit* it.)
7 He was furious. He couldn't speak.
8 The fire isn't very hot. It won't boil a kettle.
9 Tom was very foolish. He told lies to the police.
10 You are quite thin. You could slip between the bars.
11 He is very ill. He can't eat anything.
12 Our new car is very wide. It won't get through those gates.
13 The floor wasn't strong. We couldn't dance on it. (*Omit* it.)
14 I was terrified. I couldn't move.
15 The bull isn't big. He couldn't harm you.
16 The coffee isn't strong. It won't keep us awake.
17 The river is deep. We can't wade it. (*Omit* it.)

18 He is lazy. He won't get up early.
19 He won't get up early so he never catches the fast train.
20 Would you be very good and forward my letters while I am away?
21 The ice is quite thick. We can walk on it. (*Omit* it.)
22 He was very drunk. He couldn't answer my question.
23 It is very cold. We can't have breakfast in the garden.
24 He was extremely rash. He set off up the mountain in a thick fog.
25 We aren't very high. We can't see the summit.
26 You aren't very old. You can't understand these things.
27 He was very snobbish. He wouldn't talk to any of us.
28 The package is very thick. I can't push it through the letterbox.
    (*Omit* it.)
29 She was very mean. She never gave to charity.
30 He is very impatient. He never listens to anyone.
31 I was very tired. I couldn't walk any further.
32 It's not very dark. We can't see the stars clearly.
33 It was very hot. You could fry an egg on the pavement.
34 The oranges were very bitter. We couldn't eat them. (*Omit* them.)
35 Would you be very kind and turn down the radio a little?
36 He is very selfish. He wouldn't put himself out for anyone.

72 Various infinitive constructions

■ PEG 26–7, 114, 239, 249–50

Replace the group of words in italics by an infinitive or an infinitive
construction.

> It is important *that he should understand* this.
> *It is important for him to understand this.*
> He was the first man *who arrived.*
> *He was the first man to arrive.*

1 The captain was the last man *who left* the ship.
2 He got to the top *and was very disappointed when he found* that
   someone else had reached it first.
3 *The committee have decided to send you* to Paris. (You (go) to Paris,
   omit The committee have decided to send.)
4 Would you be *very* kind *and* lend me your umbrella?
5 There are a lot of sheets *that need mending.*
6 I was astonished *when I heard* that he had left the country.
7 It is better *that he should hear* it from you.
8 *I was rude* to him, *which was stupid.* (It was stupid . . .)
9 If he had another child *with whom he could play* he would be happier.
10 It is necessary *that everyone should know* the truth.
11 There was no place *where we could sit.*
12 He put his hand into his pocket *and was astonished when he found*
    that his wallet wasn't there.

13 *He rushed* into the burning house, *which* was very brave of him. (It was very brave . . .)
14 I can't go to the party; I have nothing *that I can wear.*
15 *It is expected that he will broadcast* a statement tonight. (He is expected . . .)
16 I want a kitchen *where* (= *in which*) *I can cook.*
17 He reached the station exhausted *and was very disappointed when he learnt* that the train had just left.
18 Haven't you anything *with which you could open it?*
19 *It seems that the crime was committed* by a left-handed man. (The crime seems . . . *Use perfect infinitive passive.*)
20 Is *it* likely *that he will arrive* before six? (Is he . . .)
21 I was *on the point of leaving* the house when the phone rang.
22 *This is the plan: someone will meet you* at the station . . . (You . . . (be met) at the station)
23 She is anxious *that they should have* every possible advantage.
24 *It is said that* he was a brilliant scientist. (He is said . . .)
25 The strikers decided *that the strike should continue.*
26 Would you be *very kind and translate* this for me?
27 It is advisable *that we should leave* the house separately.
28 *You signed* the document without reading it, *which was very stupid.* (It was stupid . . .)
29 *It is said that she has* a frightful temper. (She . . .)
30 He was the first man *who swam* the Channel.
31 *They believe that he is* honest. (He . . .)
32 *It appears that he was killed* with a blunt instrument. (He appears . . . *Use passive infinitive.*)
33 He was the only one *who realized* the danger.
34 *It is said that the earth was* originally part of the sun. (The earth . . .)
35 He took out his spare wheel and *was very disappointed when he discovered* that that tyre was also punctured.
36 *It is said that the murderer is hiding* in the woods near your house.

73 Perfect infinitive used with auxiliary verbs
■ PEG 255

Use the perfect infinitive of the verb in italics with the appropriate auxiliary verb. Phrases in bold type should not be repeated, but their meaning should be expressed by the auxiliary + perfect infinitive.
It is possible that he *telephoned* while we were out.
He may have telephoned while we were out.
You (*thank*) him for his present **but you didn't.**
You should have thanked him for his present.

1 I realized that my house was on fire. ~
That (*be*) a terrible moment.

Infinitive

2 I saw a ghost last night. ~
   You (*not see*) a ghost; there aren't any ghosts. You (*dream*) it.
3 **It is possible that** a child *broke* the window.
4 You *carried* it yourself, **which was not necessary.**
5 I've had a toothache for two days. ~
   You (*go*) to the dentist when it started.
6 There (*be*) motor-cycle races on the sands but as it is so wet they
   have been cancelled.
7 As I was standing in the hall your dog bit me. ~
   It (*not be*) my dog; he was with me all day. It (*be*) my brother's dog.
8 I feel terribly ill today. ~
   You (*not eat*) those mushrooms yesterday. Mushrooms don't agree
   with you.
9 I wonder why he didn't answer? ~
   Possibly he *didn't understand* the question.
10 I *gave* him a tip, **which was not necessary.**
11 The prisoner (*escape*) this way, for here are his footprints.
12 You *lied* to him, **which was wrong.**
13 I didn't recognize the voice at the other end of the line. ~
   It (*be*) my elder sister; she is often at home at that time. It (*not be*)
   my youngest sister as she is abroad.
14 Someone (*cook*) a meal here lately; the stove is still hot.
15 I've brought my own sandwiches. ~
   You (*not bring*) them. I have enough for two.
16 The burglar went straight to the safe although it was hidden behind
   a picture. ~
   Someone (*tell*) him where it was.
17 The president (*unveil*) the statue, but he is ill so his wife is doing it
   instead.
18 The plane is late; I wonder what has happened? ~
   Possibly it *was* delayed by fog.
19 I have never met him. ~
   You (*meet*) him; he lives next door to you.
20 I (*do*) it. (**It was my duty to do it, but I didn't.**)
21 He (*not catch*) the 9.20 train because he didn't leave home till 9.25.
22 I *opened* it, **which was unnecessary.**
23 The police were here while we were out. ~
   Someone (*betray*) us.
24 I *drove* at 80 miles an hour, **which was wrong.**
25 When I was your age I (*climb*) that mountain, (**but I didn't**).
26 If a policeman had seen me climbing through your window he (*ask*)
   me what I was doing.
27 He said that censorship of news was ridiculous and it (*abolish*) years
   ago. (passive verb)
28 You *boiled* so many eggs; **but** there are only four of us.
29 She (*play*) the chief part in the film, but she quarrelled with the
   director, so he engaged someone else.

30 This poem (*be*) written by Keats, **but I am not certain.**
31 He (*take*) off his hat in the theatre, **(but he didn't).**
32 People used to walk twenty miles to do their shopping. ~
    They (*have*) a lot of energy in those days.
33 One day he went for a walk up a mountain and never came back. ~
    He (*fall*) over a precipice.
34 I just pressed lightly on the pane and my hand went through. ~
    The glass (*be*) very thin.
35 You *translated* it into French, **which wasn't necessary.**
36 You *looked* at the new moon through glass. It is most unlucky.

74 Perfect infinitive used with auxiliaries and some other verbs

■ PEG 255

Instructions: as for Exercise 73, but where two verbs in italics are
placed side by side, put the second verb into the perfect infinitive
and the first into an appropriate tense.
    This palace (*say*) (*build*) in three years.
    This palace is said to have been built in three years.

1 She (*marry*) my brother but she was killed in a plane crash a month
   before the wedding date.
2 You *repeated* it, **which was unnecessary.**
3 There (*seem*) (*be*) a fight here. Everything is smashed to bits.
4 We (*set*) out today, but the weather is so bad that we decided to
   postpone our start till tomorrow.
5 I thought they were mushrooms. ~
   You (*not eat*) them unless you were sure. They (*be*) poisonous.
6 He learnt the language in six months. ~
   He (*work*) very hard.
7 I *brought* my umbrella, **which was unnecessary.**
8 I (*like*) (*bathe*) but there wasn't time.
9 I've forgotten the address. I (*write*) it down **(but I didn't).**
10 If I'd known your house was so cold I (*not come*).
11 You (*tell*) me you were going camping! If I'd known I (*go*) with
   you. ~
   But it rained all the time. You (*not like*) that, would you?
12 Who gave you my address? ~
   I don't remember. It (*be*) Tom. ~
   It (*not be*) Tom; he doesn't know it.
13 You *bought* flowers **but** we have plenty in the garden.
14 After two years of his teaching she knew absolutely nothing. ~
   He (*not be*) a good teacher.
15 My sister has just come back from abroad. She (*seem*) (*enjoy*) her trip
   very much.

Infinitive

16 Life (*be*) very uncomfortable in the Stone Age.
17 You (*stand*) still when you were being photographed, (**but you didn't**).
18 I (*go*) to a foreign university but the war prevented it.
19 I (*like*) (*photograph*) it but I had no more film.
20 There (*be*) a bad accident here. Look at all the broken glass.
21 **It is possible that** prehistoric cave drawings *were* connected with religion.
22 I have been driving for 20 years. ~
You (*not drive*) for 20 years. You are only 30 now.
23 It (*take*) years to dig the Suez Canal.
24 He walked past me without speaking. ~
He (*not recognize*) you. He is very short-sighted.
25 I (*like*) (*go*) to the match but the tickets were all sold.
26 He says he saw you at the theatre yesterday. ~
He (*not see*) me. I wasn't there.
27 This picture may be a fake; on the other hand it (*be*) painted by one of the Dutch masters.
28 **It is possible that** the fire in the ship *was started* by a bomb.
29 She walked 300 miles, carrying her child. ~
She (*have*) great courage.
30 **It is possible that** he (*read*) it in the papers. ~
He (*not read*) it. He can't read. Someone (*tell*) him.
31 I told them to meet me under the clock but they didn't turn up.
Perhaps they *were waiting* under the wrong clock. There are two in the station.
32 He told me his name was Johnson. ~
You (*mishear*) him. His name is Jones.
33 I said that I couldn't find my pen and he said that **perhaps** somebody *had borrowed* it.
34 I (*like*) (*ask*) a question but I was sitting so far back that I didn't think I'd be heard.
35 There (*be*) a fort here at one time. You can see where the foundations were.
36 The dinosaur (*be said*) (*be*) rather a stupid animal.

7 Gerund, infinitive and participles

75 The gerund

☐ PEG 257

Put the verbs in brackets into the gerund.

1 He gave up (gamble).
2 Try to avoid (make) him angry.
3 Stop (argue) and start (work).
4 The children prefer (watch) TV to (read).
5 I am against (make) any complaints.
6 It's no use (cry) over spilt milk. (*proverb*)
7 I suggest (hold) another meeting next week.
8 He finished (speak) and sat down.
9 He was fined for (drive) without lights.
10 It is difficult to get used to (eat) with chopsticks.
11 If you can't turn the key try (put) some oil in the lock.
12 He lost no time in (get) down to work.
13 You can't make an omelette without (break) eggs. (*proverb*)
14 We are looking forward to (read) your new book.
15 They escaped by (slide) down ropes made of blankets.
16 They don't allow (smoke) in here.
17 He is thinking of (leave) his job and (go) to America.
18 After (read) this article you will give up (smoke).
19 If you put your money into that business you risk (lose) every penny.
20 Imagine (live) with someone who never stops (talk).
21 Is there anything here worth (buy)?
22 He was accused of (leak) classified information to the press.
23 You'd better consult your lawyer before (decide) to buy the property.
24 I don't enjoy (go) to the dentist.
25 Would you mind (put) your pet snake somewhere else?
26 The hostages were rescued without a shot (be) fired.
27 By (work) day and night he succeeded in (finish) the job in time.
28 He has a scheme for (make) grass grow in winter.
29 I don't feel like (work); what about (go) to a disco instead?
30 Would you mind (write) your name and address on the back of the cheque?
31 If a thing is worth (do) at all it is worth (do) well. (*proverb*)

32 I hate (borrow) money.
33 He was furious at (be) mistaken for an escaped convict.
34 After (talk) for ten minutes I succeeded in (convince) him that there was no danger.
35 I remember (read) a review of that book and (think) I'd like to get it.
36 As a result of (listen) at keyholes he learnt many facts which he had no hesitation in (use) to his own advantage.

76 Gerund and infinitive

▰ PEG 266–71

Put the verbs in brackets into the correct form (gerund or infinitive).

1 I am looking forward to (see) you.
2 He dreads (have) to retire.
3 I arranged (meet) them here.
4 He urged us (work) faster.
5 I wish (see) the manager.
6 It's no use (wait).
7 He warned her (not touch) the wire.
8 Don't forget (lock) the door before (go) to bed.
9 My mother told me (not speak) to anyone about it.
10 I can't understand her (behave) like that.
11 He tried (explain) but she refused (listen).
12 At dinner she annoyed me by (smoke) between the courses.
13 You are expected (know) the safety regulations of the college.
14 He decided (disguise) himself by (dress) as a woman.
15 I am prepared (wait) here all night if necessary.
16 Would you mind (show) me how (work) the lift?
17 After (walk) for three hours we stopped to let the others (catch up) with us.
18 I am beginning (understand) what you mean.
19 He was fined for (exceed) the speed limit.
20 The boys like (play) games but hate (do) lessons.
21 I regret (inform) you that your application has been refused.
22 I couldn't help (overhear) what you said.
23 Mrs Jones: I don't allow (smoke) in my drawing-room.
   Mrs Smith: I don't allow my family (smoke) at all.
24 He surprised us all by (go) away without (say) 'Good-bye'.
25 Please go on (write); I don't mind (wait).
26 He wore dark glasses (avoid) (be) recognized.
27 Before (give) evidence you must swear (speak) the truth.
28 I tried (persuade) him (agree) with your proposal.
29 Your windows need (clean); would you like me (do) them for you?
30 Would you mind (shut) the window? I hate (sit) in a draught.
31 I can't help (sneeze); I caught a cold yesterday from (sit) in a draught.

32 Do stop (talk); I am trying (finish) a letter.
33 His doctor advised him (give up) (jog).
34 My watch keeps (stop). ~
   That's because you keep (forget) (wind) it.
35 Without (realize) it, he hindered us instead of (help) us.
36 People used (make) fire by (rub) two sticks together.

77 Gerund and infinitive

☑ PEG 266–71

Put the verbs in brackets into the correct form (gerund or infinitive).

1 He hates (answer) the phone, and very often just lets it (ring).
2 If you go on (let) your dog (chase) cars he'll end by (be) run over.
3 I prefer (drive) to (be driven).
4 I advise you (start) (look) for a flat at once.
5 Would you mind (lend) me £5? I forgot (cash) a cheque.
6 (Lie) on this beach is much more pleasant than (sit) in the office.
7 She likes her children (go) to the dentist every six months.
8 By (neglect) (take) ordinary precautions he endangered the life of his crew.
9 An instructor is coming (show) us how (use) the aqualung.
10 I have no intention of (go) to that film; I couldn't bear (see) my favourite actress in such a dreadful part.
11 I suggest (telephone) the hospitals before (ask) the police (look) for him.
12 After (hear) the conditions I decided (not enter) for the competition.
13 Some people seem (have) a passion for (write) to the newspapers.
14 He expects me (answer) by return but I have no intention of (reply) at all.
15 I tried (explain) to him but he refused (listen) and went on (grumble).
16 By (offer) enormous wages he is persuading men (leave) their present jobs and (work) for him.
17 He postponed (make) a decision till it was too late (do) anything.
18 Imagine (have) (get up) at five a.m. every day!
19 Try (forget) it; it isn't worth (worry) about.
20 There is no point in (remain) in a dangerous place if you can't do anything (help) the people who have (stay) there.
21 The horse won't be well enough (run) in tomorrow's race. He doesn't seem (have recovered) from his long journey.
22 At first I enjoyed (listen) to him but after a while I got tired of (hear) the same story again and again.
23 It is usually easier (learn) a subject by (read) books than by (listen) to lectures.
24 It wouldn't be safe (start) down now; we'll have (wait) till the mist clears.

Gerund, infinitive and participles

25 After (discuss) the matter for an hour the committee adjourned
   without (have reached) any decision.
26 It's not much use (have) a bicycle if you don't know how (ride) it.
27 He didn't dare (leave) the house because he was afraid of (meet)
   someone who might (recognize) him.
28 I distinctly remember (pay) him. I gave him £2.
29 Did you remember (give) him the key of the safe? ~
   No, I didn't. I'll go and do it now.
30 Please forgive me for (interrupt) you but would you mind (repeat)
   that last sentence?
31 I know my hair wants (cut) but I never have time (go) to the
   hairdresser's.
32 He made a lot of money by (buy) tickets in advance and (sell) them
   for twice the price on the day of the match.
33 She rushed out of the room without (give) me a chance (explain).
34 He keeps (ask) me the time and I keep (tell) him (buy) himself a
   watch.
35 He has a theory that it is possible (tell) the time in daylight by (look)
   into a cat's eyes.
36 I'd hate (be) beside a volcano when it started (erupt).

78 Gerund and infinitive

■ PEG 266–71

After **like** it is sometimes possible to use either gerund or infinitive,
but there tends to be a slight difference in implication.
like + gerund usually means 'enjoy'; it also usually implies that the
action is/was performed:
   I like skating = I enjoy skating (and do skate).
like + infinitive has more the meaning of 'approve of', 'like the idea
or habit'. In the affirmative it gives no indication as to whether the
action is performed or not, and in the negative implies that it is not
performed.
   I didn't like saying it
usually means 'I said it, unwillingly', but
   I didn't like to say it
usually means 'I didn't say it' (because it didn't seem right or
sensible). The distinction, however, is not rigid. The above notes
are, therefore, only guides which may safely be followed.

Put the verbs in brackets into gerund or infinitive.

1 I used (ride) a lot but I haven't had a chance (do) any since (come)
   here. ~
   I ride sometimes. Would you like (come) with me next time?
2 Most people prefer (spend) money to (earn) it.
3 I resented (be) unjustly accused and asked him (apologize).

116

4 It isn't good for children (eat) too many sweets.
5 I didn't feel like (work) so I suggested (spend) the day in the garden.
6 Why do you keep (look) back? Are you afraid of (be) followed?
7 Do you remember (post) the letter? ~
   Yes, I do; I posted it in the letter-box near my gate.
8 Did you remember (lock) the door? ~
   No, I didn't. I'd better (go) back and (do) it now.
9 You still have a lot (learn) if you'll forgive my (say) so.
10 It's no use (try) (interrupt) him. You'll have (wait) till he stops (talk).
11 I'm for (do) nothing till the police arrive. They don't like you (move)
   anything when a crime has been committed.
12 He didn't like (leave) the children alone in the house but he had no
   alternative as he had (go) out to work.
13 Why didn't you drink it? ~
   I didn't like (drink) it as I didn't know what it was.
14 I'm very sorry for (be) late. It was good of you (wait) for me.
15 I keep (try) (make) mayonnaise but I never succeed. ~
   Try (add) the yolk of a hard-boiled egg.
16 Do you feel like (go) to a film or would you rather (stay) at home?
17 She told me (look) through her correspondence and (take) out any
   letters that you had written her. I didn't like (look) through someone
   else's letters but I had (do) as she said.
18 He took to (get up) early and (walk) noisily about the house.
19 I liked (listen) to folk music much better than (listen) to pop.
20 The car began (make) an extraordinary noise so I stopped (see) what
   it was.
21 You'll never regret (do) a kind action.
22 He decided (put) broken glass on top of his wall (prevent) boys
   (climb) over it.
23 He annoyed me very much by (take) the piece of cake that I was
   keeping (eat) after my supper.
24 He kept (ring) up and (ask) for an explanation and she didn't know
   what (do) about him.
25 We got tired of (wait) for the weather (clear) and finally decided (set)
   out in the rain.
26 He made me (repeat) his instructions (make) sure that I understood
   what I was (do) after he had gone.
27 I suggest (leave) the car here and (send) a breakdown van (tow) it to
   the garage.
28 She apologized for (borrow) my sewing-machine without (ask)
   permission and promised never (do) it again.
29 I didn't mean (offend) anyone but somehow I succeeded in (annoy)
   them all.
30 She claimed (be able) (tell) the future by (gaze) into her crystal ball.
31 He never thinks of (get) out of your way; he expects you (walk)
   round him.
32 You don't need (ask) his permission every time you want (leave) the
   room.

Gerund, infinitive and participles

33 The police accused him of (set) fire to the building but he denied (have been) in the area on the night of the fire.
34 I left my door open. Why didn't you walk in? ~
I didn't like (go) in when you weren't there.
35 It's much better (go) to a hairdresser than (try) (save) time by (cut) your own hair.
36 I'd rather (earn) my living by (scrub) floors than (make) money by (blackmail) people.

79 Infinitive, gerund, present participle

■ PEG 266–75, 295 C, 295 D

This exercise includes examples of both **ing** forms, the gerund and the present participle. Either present participle or infinitive without **to** can be used after verbs of the senses.

Put the verbs in brackets into a correct form. When more than one form is possible it will be noted in the key.

1 When the painter felt the ladder (begin) (slip) he grabbed the gutter (save) himself from (fall).
2 The snow kept (fall) and the workmen grew tired of (try) (keep) the roads clear.
3 He offered (lend) me the money. I didn't like (take) it but I had no alternative.
4 What was in the letter? ~
I don't know. I didn't like (open) it as it wasn't addressed to me.
5 Do you remember (read) about it? ~
No, at that time I was too young (read) newspapers.
6 Did you remember (book) seats for the theatre tomorrow? ~
Yes, I have the tickets here. Would you like (keep) them? I am inclined (lose) theatre tickets.
7 Try (avoid) (be) late. He hates (be) kept (wait).
8 I didn't know how (get) to your house so I stopped (ask) the way.
9 I wish my refrigerator would stop (make) that horrible noise. You can't hear anyone (speak).
10 This book tells you how (win) at games without actually (cheat).
11 The gunman began (fire). He felt a bullet (graze) his cheek.
12 He heard the clock (strike) six and knew that it was time for him (get) up.
13 I can hear the bell (ring) but nobody seems (be coming) (open) the door.
14 Did you advise him (go) to the police? ~
No, I didn't like (give) any advice on such a difficult matter.
15 He wanted (put) my chameleon on a tartan rug and (watch) it (change) colour.

16 It is easy (see) animals on the road in daylight but sometimes at night it is very difficult (avoid) (hit) them.

17 The fire seems (be) out. ~
    It can't be quite out. I can hear the wood (crackle).

18 I caught him (climb) over my wall. I asked him (explain) but he refused (say) anything, so in the end I had (let) him (go).

19 When at last I succeeded in (convince) him that I wanted (get) home quickly he put his foot on the accelerator and I felt the car (leap) forward.

20 I'm not used to (drive) on the left. ~
    When you see everyone else (do) it you'll find it quite easy (do) yourself.

21 It is pleasant (sit) by the fire at night and (hear) the wind (howl) outside.

22 There was no way of (get) out of the building except by (climb) down a rope and Ann was too terrified (do) this.

23 We heard the engines (roar) as the plane began (move) and we saw the people on the ground (wave) good-bye.

24 It's no good (write) to him; he never answers letters. The only thing (do) is (go) and (see) him.

25 Why did you go all round the field instead of (walk) across it? ~
    I didn't like (cross) it because of the bull. I never see a bull without (think) that it wants (chase) me.

26 The people in the flat below seem (be having) a party. You can hear the champagne corks (thud) against their ceiling.

27 I don't like (get) bills but when I do get them I like (pay) them promptly.

28 Ask him (come) in. Don't keep him (stand) at the door.

29 The boys next door used (like) (make) and (fly) model aeroplanes, but they seem to have stopped (do) that now.

30 I knew I wasn't the first (arrive), for I saw smoke (rise) from the chimney.

31 We watched the men (saw) the tree and as we were walking away heard it (fall) with a tremendous crash.

32 I hate (see) a child (cry).

33 We watched the children (jump) from a window and (fall) into a blanket held by the people below.

34 It is very unpleasant (wake) up and (hear) the rain (beat) on the windows.

35 He saw the lorry (begin) (roll) forwards but he was too far away (do) anything (stop) it.

36 There are people who can't help (laugh) when they see someone (slip) on a banana skin.

80 Using participles to join sentences

◪ PEG 276–9

Join each of the following pairs of sentences, using either a present participle e.g. *knowing*, a past participle e.g. *known*, or a perfect participle e.g. *having known*. Numbers 17, 28, 33, and 36 contain three sentences each. Combine these in the same way.

> He got off his horse. He began searching for something on the ground.
> *Getting off his horse, he began searching . . .*
> I had seen photographs of the place. I had no desire to go there.
> *Having seen photographs of the place, I had no desire . . .*
> The speaker refused to continue. He was infuriated by the interruptions.
> *Infuriated by the interruptions, the speaker refused . . .*

These participle constructions are more common in written English.

1 I knew that he was poor. I offered to pay his fare.
2 We barricaded the windows. We assembled in the hall.
3 She became tired of my complaints about the programme. She turned it off.
4 He found no one at home. He left the house in a bad temper.
5 She hoped to find the will. She searched everywhere.
6 The criminal removed all traces of his crime. He left the building.
7 He realized that he had missed the last train. He began to walk.
8 He was exhausted by his work. He threw himself on his bed.
9 He had spent all his money. He decided to go home and ask his father for a job.
10 He escaped from prison. He looked for a place where he could get food.
11 She didn't want to hear the story again. She had heard it all before.
12 They found the money. They began quarrelling about how to divide it.
13 She entered the room suddenly. She found them smoking.
14 I turned on the light. I was astonished at what I saw.
15 We visited the museum. We decided to have lunch in the park.
16 He offered to show us the way home. He thought we were lost.
17 He found his revolver. He loaded it. He sat down facing the door.
18 She asked me to help her. She realized that she couldn't move it alone.
19 He fed the dog. He sat down to his own dinner.
20 He addressed the congregation. He said he was sorry to see how few of them had been able to come.
21 He thought he must have made a mistake somewhere. He went through his calculations again.
22 I have looked through the fashion magazines. I realize that my clothes are hopelessly out of date.

23 The tree had fallen across the road. It had been uprooted by the gale.
24 People were sleeping in the next room. They were wakened by the sound of breaking glass.
25 I knew that the murderer was still at large. I was extremely reluctant to open the door.
26 He stole the silver. He looked for a place to hide it.
27 We were soaked to the skin. We eventually reached the station.
28 I sat in the front row. I used opera glasses. I saw everything beautifully.
29 One evening you will be sitting by the fire. You will remember this day.
30 I didn't like to sit down. I knew that there were ants in the grass.
31 She believed that she could trust him absolutely. She gave him a blank cheque.
32 Slates were ripped off by the gale. They fell on people passing below.
33 The lion found his cage door open. He saw no sign of his keeper. He left the cage and walked slowly towards the zoo entrance.
34 The government once tried to tax people according to the size of their houses. They put a tax on windows.
35 I had heard that the caves were dangerous. I didn't like to go any further without a light.
36 She wore extremely fashionable clothes. She was surrounded by photographers and pressmen. She swept up to the microphone.

81 Misrelated participles

■ PEG 280

A participle is considered to belong to the noun or pronoun that immediately precedes it (which usually, but not necessarily, is the subject of the main verb).
    The boy, *climbing* the tree to get birds' eggs, had a bad fall.

If there is no noun/pronoun in this position the participle is considered to belong to the subject of the following main verb:
    Climbing the tree to get birds' eggs, the boy had a bad fall.
Sometimes this principle is disregarded and confusion results:
    Climbing down the tree, one of the eggs broke.
This word order makes it appear that the egg was climbing, which is nonsense. A participle linked in this way to the wrong noun/pronoun is said to be 'misrelated'. The sentence should be rewritten:
    Climbing down the tree he broke one of the eggs or
    As he was climbing down the tree one of the eggs broke.

Other examples of this type of error are given below. Correct the sentences. Sometimes only a change of order is required.

Gerund, infinitive and participles

1 When leaving a car in this car park the brakes must be left off.
2 Wading across the river, the current swept me off my feet.
3 When filling a tank with petrol naked lights should be extinguished.
4 Running into the room, a rug caught her foot and she fell.
5 Reading the letter a second time, the meaning becomes clearer.
6 When carrying a gun it should never be pointed at anyone.
7 When planting these flowers care must be taken not to damage the roots.
8 Riding in his first race, his horse fell at the last jump.
9 When paying by cheque, a bank card should be shown.
10 Knowing me to be the fool of the family, the news that I had won a scholarship astonished him.
11 Believing that his last hour had come, his hands began to tremble.
12 Passing under a ladder, a pot of paint fell on my head.
13 Reading in bed, my hands often get very cold.
14 Leaving the cinema, it seemed to him that the film had been exceptionally bad.
15 Barking furiously, I led the dog out of the room.
16 Having paid my taxes, the amount left in the bank is hardly worth mentioning.
17 Writing my name in the hotel register, a familiar voice attracted my attention.
18 Tied to a post, the sea was tossing the boat up and down.
19 Misunderstanding the question, the wrong answer was sent in.
20 Shining in the sky, we saw the first star.
21 When driving carelessly it is easy to have an accident.
22 Pinned to the door by a knife, the man saw a notice.
23 Written in large letters they read the words 'No Entry'.
24 While cleaning his gun it went off unexpectedly.
25 Wondering where to go, an advertisement caught my eye.
26 Rushing out of the house, a lorry knocked me over.
27 Sitting by the fire, it all comes back to me.
28 Falling from such a height, we thought he would never survive.
29 When changing a fuse the electricity should first be switched off.
30 Towed behind the car, I saw a trailer with a boat on it.
31 While sitting at the foot of a cliff a stone fell on him.
32 Driving to work, the traffic jams infuriated him.
33 Dropped by parachute, the country seemed entirely unfamiliar.
34 Sitting in the dentist's chair, an idea suddenly occurred to me.
35 Weakened by his last illness, I felt sure that another winter in this country would kill him.
36 Getting out of bed, a scorpion bit him.

8 Passive

82 Active to passive

☑ PEG 302-6

Put the following into the passive voice. The agent should not be mentioned except in numbers 11 and 28.

1 You should open the wine about three hours before you use it.
2 Previous climbers had cut steps in the ice.
3 Somebody had cleaned my shoes and brushed my suit.
4 We use this room only on special occasions.
5 You must not hammer nails into the walls without permission.
6 In some districts farmers use pigs to find truffles.
7 Someone switched on a light and opened the door.
8 Somebody had slashed the picture with a knife.
9 They are pulling down the old theatre.
10 Why didn't they mend the roof before it fell in?
11 The mob broke all the shop windows in recent riots.
12 The librarian said that they were starting a new system because people were not returning books.
13 The police asked each of us about his movements on the night of the crime.
14 Someone will serve refreshments.
15 People must not leave bicycles in the hall.
16 Members may keep books for three weeks. After that they must return them.
17 The burglars had cut an enormous hole in the steel door.
18 I've bought a harp. They are delivering it this afternoon. (*Do not change the first sentence.*)
19 Someone has already told him to report for duty at six.
20 They rang the church bells as a flood warning.
21 No one can do anything unless someone gives us more information.
22 People are spending far more money on food now than they spent ten years ago.
23 The organizers will exhibit the paintings till the end of the month.
24 They will say nothing more about the matter if someone returns the stolen gun.
25 It is high time someone told him to stop behaving like a child.
26 A thief stole my dog and brought him back only when I offered £20 reward for him.
27 The judge gave him two weeks in which to pay the fine.
28 They make these artificial flowers of silk.

83 Active to passive

☑ PEG 302–6

Put the following into the passive, mentioning the agent where necessary.

Where there is an indirect and a direct object, make the indirect object the subject of the passive verb.

They gave her a clock.
She was given a clock.

The gerund after certain verbs is replaced in the passive by **should be** + past participle:

They advised employing part-time workers.
They advised that part-time workers should be employed.

1 They feed the seals at the zoo twice a day.
2 Who wrote it?
3 Compare clothes which we have washed with clothes which any other laundry has washed.
4 He expected us to offer him the job.
5 They showed her the easiest way to do it.
6 Lightning struck the old oak.
7 Titian couldn't have painted it as people didn't wear that style of dress till after his death.
8 A jellyfish stung her.
9 The author has written a special edition for children.
10 Judges used to carry sweet herbs as a protection against jail-fever.
11 What did he write it with? ~
He wrote it with a matchstick dipped in blood.
12 An uneasy silence succeeded the shot.
13 Did the idea interest you?
14 The lawyer gave him the details of his uncle's will.
15 Beavers make these dams.
16 They used to start these engines by hand. Now they start them by electricity.
17 Most people opposed this.
18 Students are doing a lot of the work.
19 The Prime Minister was to have opened the dry dock.
20 They recommended opening new factories in the depressed area. (*Use* should.)
21 The closure of the workshops will make a lot of men redundant.
22 Anyone with the smallest intelligence could understand these instructions.
23 We will not admit children under sixteen.
24 Boys of sixteen to eighteen are to man this training ship.
25 A rainstorm flooded the gypsies' camp.
26 The howling of wolves kept him awake all night.
27 They suggested making the tests easier. (*Use* should.)
28 Children couldn't have done all this damage.

84 Passive to active

■ PEG 302–6

Turn the following sentences into the active voice. Where no agent is mentioned one must be supplied.

School notice: This door must be kept shut.
Students must keep this door shut.

1 Why don't you have your eyes tested? (. . . get an optician to . . . *See 119.*)
2 This speed limit is to be introduced gradually.
3 The runways are being lengthened at all the main airports.
4 It is now 6 a.m. and at most of the hospitals in the country patients are being wakened with cups of tea.
5 Byron is said to have lived on vinegar and potatoes.
6 By tradition, any sturgeon that are caught by British ships must be offered to the Queen.
7 This notice has been altered.
8 The owners went away last March and since then their houseboat has been used continuously by squatters. (*Use a continuous tense and omit* continuously.)
9 The damaged ship was being towed into harbour when the towline broke.
10 Have a lift put in and then you won't have to climb up all these stairs.
11 Last year a profit of two million pounds was made in the first six months but this was cancelled by a loss of seventeen million pounds which was made in the second six months.
12 Evening dress will be worn.
13 The ship was put into quarantine and passengers and crew were forbidden to land.
14 Someone will have to be found to take her place.
15 He was made to surrender his passport.
16 This rumour must have been started by our opponents.
17 My paintings are to be exhibited for the first time by New Arts Gallery.
18 This scientific theory has now been proved to be false.
19 The car which was blown over the cliff yesterday is to be salvaged today.
20 The house where the dead man was found is being guarded by the police to prevent it from being entered and the evidence interfered with.
21 Why wasn't the car either locked or put into the garage?
22 It is being said that too little money is being spent by the government on roads.
23 Your money could be put to good use instead of being left idle in the bank.

Passive

24 For a long time the earth was believed to be flat.
25 This copy hasn't been read. The pages haven't been cut.
26 The stones were thrown by a student, who was afterwards led away by the police.
27 Carrier pigeons are said to have been used by early Egyptian and Greek sailors.
28 The referee was being escorted from the football field by a strong police guard.

9 Indirect speech

85 Indirect speech: statements

■ PEG 307-8, 313

1 Students are asked to assume that these sentences are spoken and reported on different days. This will mean that a sentence such as: He said, 'I am coming *tomorrow*,' will become: He said that he was coming *the next day*, and so on.

This applies to all the exercises on indirect speech in this book.

2 With indirect speech, when the person addressed is mentioned, **tell** is more usual than **say to** as an introductory verb. For example:

 He told me that he was going away the next day

is more usual than

 He said to me that he was going away the next day.

Put the following into indirect speech.

1 'I have something to show you,' I said to her.
2 'Nothing grows in my garden. It never gets any sun,' she said.
3 'I'm going away tomorrow, mother,' he said.
4 'I've been in London for a month but so far I haven't had time to visit the Tower,' said Rupert.
5 'It isn't so foggy today as it was yesterday,' I remarked.
6 'The new underpass is being officially opened the day after tomorrow,' said the BBC announcer.
7 'We have moved into our new flat. We don't like it nearly so much as our last one,' said my aunt.
8 'We have a lift but very often it doesn't work,' they said.
9 'From one of the windows of my flat I can see the Eiffel Tower,' he said.
10 'I've no idea what the time is but I'll dial 8081 and find out,' said his daughter.
11 He said, 'My wife has just been made a judge.'
12 'I'll come with you as soon as I am ready,' she replied.
13 'I have a German lesson this afternoon and I haven't done my homework yet,' said the small boy.
14 'If you let the iron get too hot you will scorch your clothes,' I warned her.
15 'You haven't given me quite enough. The bill is for £14 and you've paid me only £13,' he pointed out.

16 Ann said, 'Englishmen make good husbands because they are nearly always willing to help in the house.'

17 Mary answered, 'I like men to be useful but I don't like them to be too domesticated. I prefer them to keep out of the kitchen altogether. Men look silly in aprons anyway.'

18 Motoring report: The new Rolls Royce runs so quietly that all you can hear is the ticking of the clock.
Managing director of the Rolls Royce company: In that case we'll have to do something about the clock.

19 'I don't know what to do with all my plums. I suppose I'll have to make jam. The trouble is that none of us eats jam,' she said.

20 'We like working on Sundays because we get double pay,' explained the builders.

21 He said, 'I am quite a good cook and I do all my own washing and mending too.'

22 'You can keep that one if you like, Joan,' he said. 'I've got plenty of others.'

23 'I'm going fishing with mother this afternoon,' said the small boy, 'and we are going into the garden now to dig for worms.'
(*Omit* now).

24 'You've got my umbrella,' I said crossly. 'Yours is in your bedroom.'

25 'I know exactly what they said,' the private detective explained to his client, 'because I bugged their phone.'

26 'I'll sit up till she comes in, but I hope she won't be late,' he said.

27 'If you give me some wire, I'll hang that picture for you,' said my cousin.

28 'I have a Turkish bath occasionally, but it doesn't seem to make any difference to my weight,' she said.

29 'This is quite a good model, madam. I use one of these myself,' said the salesman.

30 'My new house is supposed to be haunted, but so far I haven't seen any ghosts,' she said.

31 The advertisement said, 'If you answer the questions correctly you may win £100.'

32 'If I press my ear against the wall, I can hear what the people in the next flat are saying,' he said.

86 Indirect speech: statements

■ PEG 309-10

Some tenses/forms do not change when direct speech becomes indirect:
'I wish my children would eat vegetables,' she said.
She (said she) wished her children would eat vegetables.

Put the following into indirect speech, being careful to avoid ambiguity:

1 'I couldn't get into the house because I had lost my key, so I had to break a window,' he said.
2 'The mirror is there so that you can see yourself when you are dancing,' the instructress told him.
3 'I wrote to him the day before yesterday. I wonder why he hasn't rung up,' she said.
4 'If the ground is dry on the day of the race, my horse might win,' said the owner.
5 'You'd better slow down. There's a speed limit here,' she said to me. (*Use* advise.)
6 'If Tom wants seats, he'd better apply early,' she said.
7 'We walked 50 miles last night to see the Minister and protest about our rents being raised. He was very polite and promised to do what he could for us,' said one of the tenants.
8 'They should put traffic lights here, otherwise there'll be more accidents,' she said.
9 'It's time we began training for our next match,' the coach said to them.
10 'If you leave home at six, you should be here by nine,' he said to me.
11 'If it rains this afternoon it will be too wet to play the match tomorrow,' the captain said.
12 'I meant to plug in the electric blanket but I plugged in the electric kettle by mistake. I'm always doing silly things like that,' she told her guest.
13 'I was intending to do it tomorrow,' he said, 'but now I don't think I'll be able to.'
14 'Bill should do very well at the university, Mrs Smith,' said the headmaster. 'He's done very well here.'
15 'I don't think your father likes me,' said the young wife. 'You mustn't think that,' said her husband; 'it is just that he is old and finds it hard to get used to new people.' (*Leave* mustn't *unchanged.*)
16 'The steak is overdone again. I'm not complaining; I'm just pointing it out,' said her husband.
'I wish you'd stop pointing things out,' said his wife.
17 'They couldn't open the safe on the spot so they carried it away with them,' the night watchman reported.
18 'If you saw my father, you'd recognize him at once. He is the most extraordinary-looking man,' she said to me.
19 'I found an old Roman coin in the garden yesterday,' he said, 'and I'm going to take it to the museum this afternoon.'
20 He said, 'I got out of my boat, leaving the engine running, but while I was standing on the quay the gears suddenly engaged themselves and the boat went straight out of the harbour with no one on board.'
21 Then Macbeth enters and says, 'I have done the deed.'

22 'Would you like me to go with you?' I said.
'I'd rather go alone,' he answered.
23 My brother said, 'You may take my car if you like. I shan't be needing it tomorrow or the day after.'
24 'Yesterday Tom and I went to look at a house that he was thinking of buying. It was rather a nice house and had a lovely garden but Tom decided against it because it was opposite a cemetery,' said Celia.
25 He said, 'My wife wants to take a job but I'd rather she concentrated on our home.'
26 'I don't know what your father will say when he sees what a mess your puppies have made of this five-pound note,' said my mother.
27 'It's high time you passed your test; I'm tired of driving round with an L-plate on the front of the car,' my sister said.
28 'I wish you'd seen it,' I said to her.

87 Indirect speech: questions

☑ PEG 317

Put the following into indirect speech. The first ten questions require no change of order:
    He said, 'What is happening?'
    He asked what was happening.

1 'What happened to Mr Budd?' said one of the men.
2 'Which of his sons inherited his estate?' asked another.
3 'Who is going to live in the big house?' enquired a third.
4 'What will happen to his racehorses?' asked someone else.
5 'Which team has won?' asked Ann.
6 'Which team won the previous match?' said Bill.
7 'Who is playing next week?' he asked.
8 'Who will be umpiring that match?' asked Tom.
9 'Who wants a lift home?' said Ann.
10 'Who has just dropped a £10 note?' I asked.
11 'Where is the ticket office?' asked Mrs Jones.
12 'What shall I do with my heavy luggage?' she said. (*Use* should.)
13 'What platform does the train leave from?' asked Bill.
14 'When does it arrive in York?' he asked.
15 'When was the timetable changed?' I asked.
16 'Why has the 2.30 train been cancelled?' said Ann.
17 'How much does a day return to Bath cost?' Mrs Jones asked.
18 'Why does the price go up so often?' she wondered.
19 'How can I get from the station to the airport?' said Bill.
20 'When are you coming back?' I asked them.
21 'Is a return ticket cheaper than two singles?' said my aunt.
22 'Do puppies travel free?' asked a dog owner.

23 'Can I bring my dog into the compartment with me?' she asked.
24 'Does this train stop at York?' asked Bill.
25 'Can you telephone from inter-city trains?' said the businessman.
26 'Does the 2.40 have a restaurant car?' he enquired.
27 'Can you get coffee on the train?' asked my aunt.
28 'Do they bring it round on a trolley?' she said.
29 'Are there smoking compartments?' said the man with the pipe.
30 'Have you reserved a seat?' I asked him.

Extra exercise: read the last twenty questions, using one of the following prefaces: **I wonder/I'd like to know/Do you know?/Have you any idea?/Can you tell me?**
11 *'Do you know where the ticket office is?'*
12 *'I wonder what I should do with my heavy luggage.'*

88 Indirect speech: questions

◪ PEG 317

A new student, Paul, has come to the college and the other students are asking him questions. Imagine that he reports these questions later to an English friend:
1 *Bill asked what country I came from.*

1 'What country do you come from?' said Bill.
2 'How long have you been here?' said Ann.
3 'Are you working as well as studying?' asked Peter.
4 'Have you got a work permit?' Bill wanted to know.
5 'What are you going to study?' asked Ann.
6 'Have you enrolled for more than one class?' said Peter.
7 'Do you want to buy any second-hand books?' said Bill.
8 'Have you seen the library?' asked Ann.
9 'Do you play rugby?' said Peter.
10 'Will you have time to play regularly?' he went on.
11 'Did you play for your school team?' said Bill.
12 'Are you interested in acting?' asked Ann.
13 'Would you like to join our Drama Group?' she said.
14 'What do you think of the canteen coffee?' asked Peter.

Mary and Tom, with their son, John, aged 11, have recently come to this area. Mary wants to find a school for John and asks her neighbour Mrs Smith about the local school.
(a) Later, Mrs Smith reports these questions to her husband:
    'Is it a mixed school?'
    She asked if it was a mixed school.
(b) Alternatively, supply suitable answers to Mary's questions and then imagine that Mary reports the conversation (her questions and Mrs Smith's answers) to her husband Tom:

36 'Were your boys happy there?' ~
'Yes, they were.'
I asked if her boys had been happy there and she said that they had.

15 'How long has it been a mixed school?'
16 'Do you like the headmaster?'
17 'Is he a scientist or an arts graduate?'
18 'How many children are there in the school?'
19 'How big are the classes?'
20 'Are the classes streamed?'
21 'What is the academic standard like?'
22 'Can parents visit the school at any time?'
23 'Is there a good art department?'
24 'Do they teach music?'
25 'What instruments can the children learn?'
26 'Is there a school orchestra?'
27 'Do they act plays?'
28 'What sort of plays have they done?'
29 'What games do they play?'
30 'Are the playing fields near the school?'
31 'Are they taught to swim?'
32 'Can the children get dinner at school?'
33 'Is the food good?'
34 'Is there a Parent-Teacher Association?'
35 'How often does it meet?'
36 'Were your own boys happy at the school?'

89 Indirect speech: questions

☑ PEG 317

Put the following into indirect speech.

1 'Why are you looking through the keyhole?' I said.
2 'Who put salt in my coffee?' he asked.
3 'Which of you knows how to make Irish stew?' said the chief cook.
4 'Why did you travel first class?' I asked him.
5 'How can I run in high-heeled shoes?' she enquired.
6 'What is your new house like?' I asked them.
7 He said, 'Where am I supposed to go now?' (*Omit* now.)
8 'Whose car did you borrow last night?' I said to him.
9 'What was she wearing when you saw her last?' the policeman asked me.
10 'Who owns this revolver?' said the detective.
11 'Where were you last night, Mr Jones?' he said.
12 'What else did you see?' I asked the boy.
13 'Have you done this sort of work before?' said his new employer.

14 'Can you read the last line on the chart?' the oculist asked her.
15 'Did they understand what you said to them?' he asked me.
16 'Are you being attended to, sir?' said the shop assistant.
17 'Will you go on strike when the others do?' the shop steward
   asked him.
18 'Do you see what I see, Mary?' said the young man.
19 'Who left the banana skin on the front doorstep?' said my mother.
20 'Have you gone completely mad?' I asked. 'Do you want to blow us
   all up?'
21 'Why is your house so full of antiques?' she asked. 'Was your father
   a collector?'
22 'Are you leaving today or tomorrow morning?' said his secretary.
23 'How far is it?' I said, 'and how long will it take me to get there?'
24 'Could I speak to Mrs Pitt?' said the caller.
   'I'm afraid she's out,' said the *au pair* girl. 'Could I take a message?'
25 'Are you sorry for what you did?' the mother asked the little boy.
26 'Are you going to see him off at the station?' I asked her.
27 'Would you mind if I looked inside your bag, Madam?' said the
   policeman.
28 'If someone fell at your feet foaming at the mouth would you know
   what to do?' said the instructor in First Aid.
29 'Why do you think it may be dangerous?' he asked her.
30 'Do you know that the shoes you are wearing aren't a pair?' I asked
   him.

90 Indirect speech: commands, requests, advice expressed by object + infinitive

◢ PEG 320

Indirect commands, requests, etc. are normally expressed by **tell,
order, ask, beg, advise, remind, warn**, etc., with the person
addressed and the infinitive. Change the following direct commands
into indirect commands using this construction. Remember that the
person addressed is often not mentioned in a direct command:
   He said, 'Go away',
but must be mentioned in an indirect command:
   He told me (Tom/us/them, etc.) to go away.

1 'Switch off the TV,' he said to her.
2 'Shut the door, Tom,' she said.
3 'Lend me your pen for a moment,' I said to Mary.
4 'Don't watch late-night horror movies,' I warned them.
5 'Don't believe everything you hear,' he warned me.
6 'Please fill up this form,' the secretary said.
7 'Don't hurry,' I said.
8 'Don't touch that switch, Mary,' I said.

9 'Open the safe!' the raiders ordered the bank clerk.
10 'Please do as I say,' he begged me.
11 'Help your mother, Peter,' Mr Pitt said.
12 'Don't make too much noise, children,' he said.
13 'Do whatever you like,' she said to us.
14 'Don't miss your train,' she warned them.
15 'Read it before you sign it,' he said to his client.
16 'Do sing it again,' he said.
17 'Don't put your hands near the bars,' the zoo keeper warned us.
18 'Buy a new car,' I advised him.
19 'Don't drive too fast,' she begged him.
20 'Don't lean your bicycles against my windows, boys,' said the shopkeeper.
21 'Come to the cinema with me,' he asked her.
22 'Cook it in butter,' I advised her.
23 'Don't touch the gates, madam,' said the lift operator.
24 'Don't argue with me,' the teacher said to the boy.
25 'Pull as hard as you can,' he said to him.
26 'Send for the Fire Brigade,' the manager said to the porter.
27 'Don't lend her anything,' he advised us.
28 'Make a list of what you want,' she told us.
29 'Look at the paper,' he said to her.
30 'Stand clear of the doors,' a voice warned the people on the platform.
31 'See if you can find any mushrooms, children,' she said.
32 'Don't go alone,' I warned her.
33 'Pay at the cash desk,' the shop assistant said to the customer.
34 The notice said, 'Leave this space clear.'
35 'Remember to write to your mother,' I said to them.
36 'Think well before you answer,' the detective warned her.

91 Indirect speech: commands, requests, advice

☐ PEG 320

See note to 90.

Put the following into indirect speech. In most cases the person addressed must be supplied.

1 He said, 'Get out of my way.'
2 'Climb in through the window,' he ordered.
3 'Please pay at the desk,' said the assistant.
4 'Open your bag, please,' said the store detective.
5 'Don't worry about anything, Mrs Pitt,' said her solicitor. 'Leave it all to me.'
6 'Don't use bent coins in a slot machine,' I warned him.
7 'Follow that car,' the detective said to the taxi-driver.

8 'Wash it in lukewarm water,' recommended the assistant.
9 'Have confidence in me,' urged the doctor.
10 'Take me up to the 33rd floor,' he said to the liftman.
11 'Read the notice about life-saving equipment,' advised the air-hostess.
12 'Always cook with butter,' said her mother, 'never use margarine.'
13 'Don't argue with your father,' I said.
14 'Remember to prune the roses,' said my aunt.
15 'Wait for me at the bridge,' said the young man.
16 'Don't eat too much starch,' I advised her, 'and avoid fried food.'
17 'Don't say anything to make her angry,' said my father.
18 Notice: Please do not ask at the desk for change for telephone calls.
19 'Don't forget to feed the goldfish,' Mary said to her brother.
20 'Cross the line by the footbridge,' said the porter.
21 'Write to me as often as you can,' said his wife.
22 'Put your pistol on the table,' said the crook.
23 'Please book me a seat in a non-smoker,' said the traveller.
24 'Don't forget your sandwiches,' said his mother.
25 'Don't go near the water, children,' she said.
26 'Search the house,' said the police sergeant.
27 'Don't make mountains out of molehills,' he said.
28 'Put down that gun. It's loaded,' she warned.

92 Indirect speech: commands, requests, advice

☑ PEG 320

See note to 90.

Put the following into indirect speech, joining the sentences together with **as, and, but** or **for**.

1 'Make good use of your time. You won't get such an opportunity again,' he said to us.
2 'Don't wait till tomorrow,' said the advertisement, 'post the coupon at once.'
3 'Be very careful crossing roads,' she said, 'and remember to drive on the right.'
4 'I can't open it. You have a try, Peter,' he said.
5 'Go and get me a paper, and come straight back,' he said to me.
6 'Someone's coming. Get into the cupboard,' she said.
7 'Give way to traffic approaching from your right,' the road sign warned us.
8 'Please, please send whatever you can spare,' said the secretary of the disaster fund.
9 'Wear a wig if you don't want to be recognized,' I advised him.
10 'Don't bathe when the red flag is flying,' said the lifeguard.

Indirect speech

11 'Don't forget to thank Mrs Jones when you are saying goodbye to her,' said his mother.
12 'Watch the milk and don't let it boil over,' he said.
13 'Don't shelter under a tree in a thunderstorm,' he said. 'The tree might be struck by lightning.'
14 'Put the message into a bottle and throw it into the sea,' he said.
15 'Read it for yourself if you don't believe what I say,' he told me.
16 'Don't forget to use your indicators,' said the driving instructor.
17 'Don't drive too fast or the baby'll be sick,' she said to her husband.
18 'Do make the coffee a bit stronger,' I begged. 'It was terribly weak last night.'
19 'Beware of pickpockets,' said a huge notice.
20 'Smell this. Do you think it has gone bad?' she said.
21 'Don't take your coat off. We are going out again in a moment,' she told him.
22 'Stand by the window and tell me if anyone goes into the house opposite,' he said.
23 'Don't move till the policeman waves you on,' said the driving instructor.
24 'Don't touch it. You will only make it worse,' he told me.
25 'Be careful; the steps are very slippery,' I warned him.
26 'Ask your boss to ring me back,' I said. 'My number is 1234567.' 'Could you repeat that, please?' said the girl.
27 'Don't work too fast,' said the foreman. 'If we finish before six we shan't get any overtime.'
28 'Prepare to meet your doom. The end of the world is at hand,' said the placard.
29 'Remember to put the brake on,' the instructor said.
30 'Would you please take off your shoes?' Keiko said to him.

93 Indirect speech: commands, requests, invitations, offers, advice

■ PEG 284–7, 318–20

Put the following into indirect speech using **ask, advise, invite, offer remind, tell, warn.**

1 'Would you like to have lunch with me on Sunday?' he said to me.
2 'Would you like a cigarette?' said one of the guests.
3 'Would you mind not smoking between courses?' said their hostess.
4 'Take these letters to the post, will you? And shut the door as you go out,' said the boss.
5 'Will you help me, please?' she said. 'I can't reach the top shelf.'
6 'This is a horrible room. Why don't you ask for something better?' he said.
7 'If I were you I'd try to get a room on the top floor,' he said.

8 'I'll wait for you if you like,' she said.
9 'Remember to switch off when you've finished,' he said.
10 'You might check these figures for me,' he said.
11 'You'd better apologize for being late,' said my mother.
12 'Could you check the oil, please?' I asked the mechanic.
13 'I wish you'd sit still!' said the artist. 'How do you expect me to paint you when you keep jerking your head?'
14 'Why don't you go by train? It's much less tiring than driving,' I said.
15 Hotel notice: Will guests please not play radios loudly after midnight?
16 'Would you like to wait here?' said the receptionist, showing me into the waiting room.
17 'You must see this exhibition!' said all my friends.
18 'I should plant daffodils, if I were you,' I said to them.
19 'If you'd just sign the back of the cheque,' said the bank clerk.
20 'I'd be very grateful if you'd forward my letters while I am away,' he said.
21 Police announcement: Will anyone who saw this accident please get in touch with their nearest police station?
22 'Don't leave your room at night,' he said. 'Our host's dogs might mistake you for a burglar.'
23 'Answer this letter for me, will you?' he said. 'And remember to keep a copy.'
24 'Would you mind moving your car?' he said. 'It's blocking my gate.'
25 (in a letter) 'Perhaps you'd let me know when your new stock comes in.' (*Mrs Jones . . .*)
26 Notice on board: The first team will report to the gymnasium for weight-training. (*The coach . . .*)
27 'Could you sew on this button for me?' Tom asked Ann. 'You'd better sew it on yourself,' said Mary. 'Buttons sewn on by Ann usually come off the next day.'
28 'If you will kindly sit down the fortune-teller will be with you in a moment,' the girl said.

94 Indirect speech: questions, requests, invitations, offers, advice

■ PEG 284–7, 318–20, 323

Remember that **Why don't you?** can be an ordinary question or advice/suggestion. Treat it here as advice.

Put the following into indirect speech.

1 'Could you get there and back in one day?' I asked. (*I asked if he . . .*)
2 'I can't open this tin,' said Ann. 'Shall I do it for you?' said Tom.
3 'Could you translate this for me, please?' I asked the official.

4 'Shall we ever meet again?' he wondered.

5 'Will you be here tomorrow?' she asked. 'Yes,' I answered.

6 'Could I lose five kilos in a week?' said the fat woman. 'No,' said the doctor.

7 'Will you have a drink?' he said.

8 'Why don't you install gas central heating?' said the advertisement. (*urge*)

9 'Will you read this very carefully, please?' he said to me.

10 'Shall I tell him what happened?' she asked me.

11 'Wouldn't you like to look ten years younger?' said the hairdresser.

12 'I'm going to Brighton tomorrow,' said Ann.
'So'm I,' said Tom. 'Would you like a lift?' (*Tom said he was too and . . .*)

13 'Can I have a sweet?' said the small boy.

14 'Can we stay up till the end of the programme?' said the children.

15 'Could I have the weekend off?' he asked his boss.

16 'Could I leave early on Friday?' he said.

17 'Why don't you like pop music?' the teenagers asked him.

18 'Why don't you take up the oboe again?' said my friends. (*advise*)

19 'Where shall I hang my new picture?' he said. 'Would it look well over the mantelpiece?'

20 'What shall I do if the car won't start?' I said.

21 'Have you got enough money? Shall I lend you some?' said my friend.

22 'Will you be able to guide me or shall I bring a map?' I asked.

23 'You won't forget to shut the door, will you?' she said. (*remind*)

24 'Would you like to see over the house?' I asked her.

25 'Would you like to peel the potatoes?' said Ann, handing me a knife.

26 'I've got two tickets. Would you like to come with me?' he said.

27 'Can you use a word processor?' he asked. 'No,' I said.

28 'Would you mind living by yourself for six months?' they asked.

29 'Would you mind paying cash?' said my landlady when I took out my cheque-book.

30 'Why don't you trust him?' I asked Ann.
'I never trust left-handed men,' she answered.

95 Indirect speech: commands and questions with if- clauses and time clauses

☑ PEG 229, 320–1

Questions with **if-** clauses and time clauses should be reported with the **if-** clause or time clause last.

'When/If I see him, what shall I say?' she asked.
She asked what she should say when/if she saw him.

Commands can be reported by **tell** + infinitive + **if-** clause/time clause.

But sometimes (as in nos. 5 and 10 below) this would produce a rather clumsy sentence. It is then advisable to use **say/said that** + **if**-clause/time clause + **be/should** + infinitive:

'If /When you see him, ask him to ring me,' she said.
She said that if/when I saw him I was to ask him to ring her.
was to expresses a definite command; **should** implies advice.

Put the following into indirect speech.

1 He said, 'When you are at the butcher's remember to get a bone for the dog.'
2 She said, 'If you feel faint sit down and put your head between your knees.'
3 'If I find your purse what shall I do with it?' he said.
   'Keep it till you see me again,' I replied.
4 She said, 'If he arrives before I get back give him something to drink.'
5 'If anyone rings up,' she said, 'say that I'll be back shortly.'
6 'When you are driving always look in your driving mirror before turning right,' said my instructor.
7 'Leave the key under the mat if you go out,' she said.
8 'If you think the room is cold shut the windows,' said my aunt.
9 'If you feel lonely any time ring me up,' he said.
10 'If she doesn't eat meat, offer her an omelette,' he said.
11 'Get the car off the road on to the verge if you have a puncture. Don't leave it on the road,' said my father.
12 'If I am not back by this time tomorrow take this letter to the police,' he said.
13 'When you see Mrs Pitt don't forget to thank her,' she said to her husband.
14 'When the bell rings take the meat out of the oven,' my sister said.
15 'If you are taken prisoner,' said the officer, 'give your name, rank and number but refuse to answer any other questions.'
16 'When you hear the fire alarm, shut all windows and go downstairs as quickly as possible,' said the schoolmaster.
17 'If the lift should stop between two floors press the emergency button,' he said.
18 'Before you allow anyone to use the Turkish bath remember to ask him if he has a weak heart,' said the senior attendant.
19 'If the police stop me, what shall I say?' she asked.
20 'What shall I do if he refuses to let me in?' she said.
   'Write a note and push it under the door,' I said.
21 'What will happen if the strike continues?' he said.
22 'If it goes on snowing, how'll we get food?' wondered the housewives.
23 'When the rain stops, can we go out?' said the children.
24 'When you've completed one section, go on to the next,' the teacher said.

25 'If you don't like the programme, switch to another channel,' I said to her.
26 'If I lose my traveller's cheques, will the bank repay me?' I asked.
27 'If the noise gets worse, you'd better complain to the police,' he said to me.
28 'As soon as you find a hotel, ring me and give me the address,' he said.

96 Indirect speech: suggestions

◢ PEG 289 D, 322

Part 1 Write the following in indirect speech, in ordinary narrative form.

Ann suggested having a party on the next Saturday. Mary agreed and asked who they should invite.

Report 'Why don't we . . . ?' as a suggestion and 'Why don't you . . ?' as suggestion or advice. Report 'Why not?' in no. 9 as *agreed*.

1 Ann: What about having a party on Saturday?
2 Mary: Yes, let's. Who shall we invite?
3 Ann: Let's not make a list. Let's just invite everybody.
4 Mary: We don't want to do too much cooking, so what about making it a wine and cheese party?
5 Ann: Suppose we ask everybody to bring a bottle?
6 Mary: Shall we hire glasses from our local wine shop? We haven't many left.
7 Ann: If it's warm, how about having the party in the garden?
8 Mary: Why not have a barbecue?
9 Ann: Why not? We could ask Paul to do the cooking.
10 Mary: Last time we had a barbecue the neighbours complained about the noise. Shall we ask everyone to speak in whispers?
11 Ann: Suppose we go round to the neighbours and apologize in advance this time?
12 Mary: Why not invite the neighbours? Then the noise won't matter.
13 Ann: What a clever idea! Shall we start ringing everyone up tonight?
14 Mary: What about working out how much it will cost first?

Part 2 Put the following into indirect speech.

15 'What about a round-the-world cruise?' suggested Mrs Smith. 'What about renting a caravan? It's all we can afford,' said her husband.
16 'Suppose you complain, Ann?' I said. 'The boss is more likely to listen to you than to any of us.'
17 'You used to be a good tennis player,' she reminded him. 'Why don't you take it up again?'

18 'Shall we talk there? It's not far,' he said. 'Yes, let's,' I said.
19 'What about joining a weaving class?' Ann said to me. 'There's one starting soon.'
20 'Let's organize a sponsored cycle race,' said the children.
   'What about a sponsored silence?' said the teacher with a grin.
21 'Where shall we meet?' I said. 'What about the hotel?' said Bill.
22 'Suppose you ring him, Ann, and ask him what he thinks of the idea?' I said.
23 'I'm doing most of the work,' I pointed out. 'What about giving me a hand?'
24 'Let's leave the washing-up till tomorrow,' he suggested. 'I hate washing up last thing at night.'
25 'Suppose the children go on an adventure holiday this summer?' suggested the father.
26 'Why don't you ask them what they'd like to do?' I said.
27 'Shall we begin training for the next London Marathon?' said Bill. 'I've no intention of running in marathons,' I said. 'Why don't you ask Paul?'
28 'Why don't you put an advertisement in the local paper?' they suggested to me.

97 Indirect speech: mixed types

■ PEG chapter 31 (note especially 324)

Put the following into indirect speech, avoiding as far as possible the verbs **say**, **ask** and **tell** and choosing instead from the following:
accept, accuse, admit, advise, agree, apologize, assure, beg, call
(= summon), **call** (+ noun/pronoun + noun), **complain, congratulate, deny, exclaim, explain, give, hope, insist, introduce, invite, offer, point out, promise, protest, refuse, remark, remind, suggest, thank, threaten, warn, wish.**

1 He said, 'Don't walk on the ice; it isn't safe.'
2 'Miss Brown, this is Miss White. Miss White, Miss Brown,' he said.
3 'Here are the car keys. You'd better wait in the car,' he said to her.
4 'Please, please, don't tell anyone,' she said.
   'I won't, I promise,' I said.
5 'Would you like my torch?' I said, holding it out.
   'No, thanks,' he said. 'I have one of my own.' (*Omit* thanks)
6 Tom: I'll pay.
   Ann: Oh no, you mustn't!
   Tom: I insist on paying!
7 'Come in and look round. There's no obligation to buy,' said the shopkeeper.
8 'If you don't pay the ransom, we'll kill the boy,' said the kidnappers.
9 'I won't answer any questions,' said the arrested man.

10 'He expects a lot of work for very little money,' complained one of the typists.
   'Yes, he does,' agreed the other.
11 'I wish it would rain,' she said.
12 'You pressed the wrong button,' said the mechanic. 'Don't do it again. You might have a nasty accident.'
13 'Your weight's gone up a lot!' I exclaimed.
   'I'm afraid it has,' she said sadly.
14 'I hope you'll have a good journey,' he said. 'Don't forget to send a card when you arrive.'
15 'Hurrah! I've passed the first exam!' he exclaimed.
   'Congratulations!' I said, 'and good luck with the second.'
16 'All right, I'll wait a week,' she said. (*Omit* all right)
17 'Many happy returns of your birthday!' we said.
   'Thanks,' said the boy.
18 'Your door is the shabbiest in the street,' said the neighbour.
   'It is,' I said.
19 'Cigarette?' ~
   'Thanks,' I said.
20 'I'll sell the TV set if you keep quarrelling about the programme,' said their mother.
   'No, don't do that! We won't quarrel any more,' said the children.
21 'I'll give you £500 to keep your mouth shut,' he said to me.
22 'I'll wait for you, I promise,' he said to me.
23 'I'm sorry I'm late,' she said. 'The bus broke down.'
24 'You've been leaking information to the Press!' said his colleagues.
   'No, I haven't,' he said. 'Liar!' said Tom.
25 'I'll drop you from the team if you don't train harder,' said the captain.
26 'If the boys do anything clever, you call them your sons,' complained his wife. 'But if they do anything stupid, you call them mine.'
27 'Let's have a rest,' said Tom.
   'Yes, let's,' said Ann.
28 'Ugh! There's a slug in my lettuce. Waiter!' he cried.

98 Indirect to direct speech

■ PEG 307–22

Put the following into direct speech, using dialogue form:
   Tom: *Would you like to come for a drive tomorrow, Ann?*
   Ann: *I'd love to* etc.

Trip to Stratford

1 Tom invited Ann to come for a drive the following day.
2 Ann accepted with pleasure and asked where he was thinking of going.

3 He said he'd leave it to her.
4 She suggested Stratford . . .
5 adding that she hadn't been there for ages.
6 Tom agreed and said that they might go on the river if it was a fine day.
7 Ann wondered what was on at the Royal Shakespeare Theatre.
8 Tom said they'd find out when they got there . . .
9 adding that it was usually possible to get seats on the day of the play.
10 He asked Ann if she could be ready by ten.
11 Ann said with regret that she couldn't as she had to type a report first.
12 Tom expressed horror at the idea of working on Saturday . . .
13 and advised her to change her job.
14 She told him not to be ridiculous and explained that . . .
15 she had volunteered to type the report in return for a free afternoon the following week.
16 She pointed out that she hadn't known that he was going to ask her out.
17 Tom said he supposed it was all right but . . .
18 warned her not to make a habit of volunteering for weekend work.
19 Ann promised not to.
20 Tom said gloomily that he supposed she'd be busy all morning.
21 Ann assured him that she'd be finished by 11.00 and . . .
22 offered to meet him at the bus stop at Hyde Park Corner.
23 Tom said that it wasn't a very good meeting place and that he'd call for her.
24 Ann said that that was very kind of him and that she'd be waiting in the hall.

Hill climb

25 Tom suggested climbing to the top, adding that the view from there was marvellous . . .
26 but Ann said that they'd been climbing for three hours and that she was too tired to go any further.
27 She suggested that Tom should go on up while she went down and waited there.
28 Tom agreed and handed her the car keys, advising her to wait in the car.
29 He promised to be as quick as he could.
30 Ann said that if he was too long there'd be no lunch left, for she'd have eaten it all.

10 Purpose

99 Infinitive used to express purpose

■ PEG 334

Combine each of the following pairs of sentences into one sentence using **so as/in order** where necessary.

> He sent me to Spain. He wanted me to learn Spanish.
> *He sent me to Spain to learn Spanish.*
> He turned out the light. He didn't want to waste electricity.
> *He turned out the light so as not to waste electricity.*

1 I am buying paint. I want to paint my hall door.
2 He tied a knot in his handkerchief. He hoped that this would remind him to meet the train.
3 He opened the lions' cage. He intended to feed the lions.
4 He left his rifle outside. He didn't want to frighten his wife.
5 He has a box. He plans to put his savings in it. (*Omit* it.)
6 We had no cups but he gave us coconut shells. He said we could drink out of them. (*Omit* them.)
7 He rushed into the burning house. He wanted to save the child.
8 He read only for short periods each day. He didn't want to strain his eyes.
9 They got up very early. They wanted to get to the top of the hill before sunrise.
10 He rang the bell. He wanted to tell us that dinner was ready.
11 We must keep our gloves on. We don't want to get frost-bitten.
12 The farmer put a scarecrow up in the field. He wanted to frighten the birds.
13 I took off my shoes. I didn't want to make any noise.
14 Before the carpenter came she covered the floor with polythene sheeting. She wanted to protect the carpet.
15 The boys are collecting sticks. They intend to put them on the fire. (*Omit* them.)
16 He was playing very softly. He didn't want to disturb anyone.
17 I am sending him to the USA. I want him to study electronics there.
18 I sent him out of the room. I wanted to discuss his progress with his headmaster.
19 He fixed a metal ladder to the wall below his window. He wanted to be able to escape if there was a fire.
20 He changed his address constantly. He wanted to elude the police.
21 The police have barricaded the main streets. They want to prevent the demonstrators from marching through the town.

22 They evacuated everybody from the danger zone. They wanted to reduce the risk.
23 I am learning Greek. I wish to read Homer.
24 He sent his children to his sister's house. He wanted them to watch the television programme.
25 He sent his children to their aunt's house. He wanted to have some peace.
26 The town council has forbidden coal fires. They are trying to keep the air clean.
27 They employed a detective. They wanted to learn what I did in the evenings.
28 I am saving up. I want to buy a helicopter.
29 He coughed. He wanted to warn them that he was coming.
30 You should take your holidays in June. In this way you would avoid the rush.
31 I keep my hens in a field surrounded by wire netting. I want to protect them against the foxes.
32 I am learning skiing at an indoor school. I want to be able to ski when I get to Switzerland.
33 The workmen left red lights near the hole. They wanted to warn motorists.
34 He invented a wife and six children. By this trick he hoped to avoid paying income tax.
35 Some women tint their hair when it goes grey. They want to look younger.
36 He didn't tell her he was going up in the spacecraft. He didn't want to alarm her.

100 Clauses and phrases of purpose

■ PEG 336-7

A purpose clause introduced by **so that** can sometimes be replaced by **prevent/avoid** + gerund or **allow/enable/let/make** etc. + infinitive.

The two sentences:
> He rumpled the bedclothes. He wanted to make me think he had slept in the bed.
could be combined:
> *He rumpled the bedclothes so that I should/would think he had slept* etc. or *to make me think he had slept* etc.
An **in case** clause is useful when we mention the possible future action we are taking precautions against:
> Don't let him play with scissors. He may cut himself.
could be expressed:
> *Don't let him play with scissors in case he cuts himself.*

Purpose

Sometimes an **in case** clause can be replaced by a negative purpose clause.

1 He killed the men who helped him to bury the treasure. He wanted nobody but himself to know where it was.
2 Put the cork back. Someone may knock the bottle over.
3 The airfield authorities have put arc lights over the damaged runway.
They want repair work to continue day and night.
4 The girl packed the vase in polyester foam. She didn't want it to get broken in the post.
5 He wore a false beard. He didn't want anyone to recognize him.
6 She built a high wall round her garden. She didn't want her fruit to be stolen.
7 They talked in whispers. They didn't want me to overhear them.
8 You ought to take some serum with you. You may get bitten by a snake.
9 Aeroplanes carry parachutes. The crew can escape in case of fire.
10 I am insuring my life. I want my children to have something to live on if I am killed.
11 Please shut the gate. I don't want the cows to get out of the field.
12 He telephoned from a public call-box. He didn't want the call to be traced to his own address.
13 I am putting nets over my strawberry plants. I don't want the birds to eat all the strawberries.
14 We keep a spade in the house. There may be a heavy fall of snow in the night.
15 We put bars on the lower windows. We didn't want anyone to climb in.
16 You should carry a jack in your car. You may have a puncture.
17 We built the roof with a steep slope. We wanted the snow to slide off easily.
18 The notices are written in several languages. The government wants everyone to understand them.
19 I put my address on my dog's collar. I want anyone who finds him to know where he comes from.
20 She tied a bell round her cat's neck. She wanted the birds to know when he was approaching.
21 Bring your gun with you. We may be attacked.
22 I have put wire over my chimney-pots. I don't want birds to build nests in them.
23 Write your name in the book. He may forget who lent it to him.
24 He chained up the lioness at night. He didn't want her to frighten anyone.
25 Don't put on any more coal. The chimney may catch fire.
26 The burglar cut the telephone wires. He didn't want me to call the police.
27 Take a torch with you. It may be dark before you get back.

28 The manufacturers have made the taps of their new gas cooker very stiff. They don't want young children to be able to turn them on.

29 Don't let the baby play with my glasses. He may break them.

30 The debate on education has been postponed. The government want to discuss the latest crisis.

31 If someone knocks at the door at night don't open it. It may be the escaped convict.

32 The policeman stopped the traffic every few minutes. He wanted the pedestrians to be able to cross the road.

33 He had a telephone installed in his car. He wanted his secretary to be able to contact him whenever necessary.

34 Never let children play with matches. They may set themselves on fire.

35 As he went through the forest Bill marked the trees. He wanted the rest of the party to know which way he had gone.

36 Turn down the oven. We don't want the meat to burn while we are out.

Key

1 Articles

Exercise 1 (note that '–' indicates that no article is required.)
1 a, –   2 –, –, –; a   3 a, a   4 a, –; a; a, –   5 A, –, –   6 –, a, an
7 A,   –,   a, a, –, a   8 –, –; a, –   9 A, –   10 a, a; a, an   11 a, a; –; a,
–, a   12 –, an,   an; –   13 a, a; a; a, a   14 –, an   15 A, a; a; a, a
16 an, a; –, an, –, a, a   17 a, –; a, –   18 –, a   19 a; a, –   20 a, a; a;
–   21 A; a, an; a   22 –, a, an,   a   23 –, a, an   24 a, –; a   25 a; a, a
26 a, a; –   27 an, a, –, –   28 –; –   29 a, a, –, –   30 an; a, a, a; a; –
31 a, a; an, a   32 a, a, a, a   33 –, a, a   34 a, a   35 a, a   36 –, a

Exercise 2 (As before '–' indicates that no article is required. '(the)'
indicates that the article is optional.)

1 The, –, the, –   2 the; the, the   3 –, –, –, the   4 –, –   5 the; the,
the; –   6 –, –, –; the, the, –; the   7 the, the; –, –   8 –, –, the   9 –;
–, –   10 the,   the; the   11 –, –; the, the; the   12 the, the, the, the,
–   13 –, –, –   14 –,   –, –, –   15 –, –, the   16 –, –, –, the   17 –,
the, the, –   18 –, –   19 –, –,   –, –, –   20 the, the, the   21 the, –;
–, the   22 The,   –; the; –, –, –   23 –;   the, the, the   24 –; –; the
25 –, the, –, the   26 –,   –, –, the, the; The, –, the; the, the, the,
the, –, the, the   27 –, the, the; –   28 the, the; The, the, the, the
29 –, –, the, the, –, –   30 –, –, –; –, –   31 –, –, the, –   32 The,
–; –, –, the   33 –, (the), the, the, the   34 (the), (the); –, –, –, –, the
35 –,   –   36 the, the, the, the, the, the

Exercise 3 (Two words separated by an oblique, e.g. the/his, indicate
that either is a possible answer. The first word is normally the
preferred answer.)

1 a, the; a, a   2 an, the, the   3 a, the, –, –   4 the, a, the, –, –, (the)
5 a, –, the, a   6 a, a/the, an, the   7 a, –, an, the, the, the, the   8 a,
the, the   9 a, a   10 the, the, the, the, an   11 –, –, (the), a   12 a, the,
–   13 the, a, the, the, the   14 –; –, –, –   15 The, the, the; the, the
16 the, the, a, –; (the), the, the, –   17 a   18 a; the; a; a   19 a, the; a,
–; The, the   20 –, the; the; a, an 21 The, a, a, –, –   22 the, a, –, the,
a, the, the, the, the   23 a, a, a, the, –, the; The, –, –; The, the, –; –,
the, –, an   24 the, the, a   25 a, the, the   26 –, the; the; –, the; –, a,
–   27 a, the, the, –   28 a, –, an   29 –, –,   –, –   30 a, an, an, a; –,
–, –, –, the   31 a; the, the, the; a, –   32 the, an, the;   –, the, –; the,
the, a   33 –, –; the   34 –; a, the, –, a   35 –, the; a   36 a, a, a, the;
the, the, –

Exercise 4 1 his 2 your, your 3 –, their 4 the 5 his, his 6 his,
– 7 an, the 8 a 9 a, my 10 the 11 a, –, a, his, – 12 his 13 –,
her 14 his 15 the 16 our 17 the, her 18 his 19 your 20 his, the
21 the 22 your 23 –, his 24 –, our/the 25 his 26 the/his 27 your,
the, the 28 a 29 a 30 a, a 31 your, (a) 32 her, the 33 a, his
34 your 35 your 36 my

Exercise 5 1 One, a, a 2 A, a; one; a; one, a; a; a 3 A, a 4 a, a,
an 5 a, a/the, a/your 6 one; a; an 7 a, a 8 One, a 9 (a), a, a; a;
One 10 a; One 11 a/the; a, a/the; – 12 a, a, one 13 one; one; a
14 a; a, a 15 a, one, a, a, a 16 a, a; one 17 One, a, a 18 –, a; a;
one, a: A, a 19 a; a 20 One; an, an 21 a, a/the, a; a, a, an 22 One,
a, –, an 23 One, a, –, a, a 24 one; a; a; a; One, an; a

2 Auxiliary verbs

Exercise 6 Negative answers in each case: the auxiliary verb + **not**.
not is usually contracted and added to the verb, e.g. may not/mayn't
cost. **will** + **not** is contracted to **won't**. **can** + **not** is contracted to
can't.

Interrogative answers, except for 1, 13 and 19, are in the following
form: auxiliary verb + subject + infinitive, e.g. Should they eat less?
    1 Is it likely to cost/Do you think it will cost? 13 Are they likely to
come/Do you think they will come? 19 Is he likely to be at home/Do
you think he'll be at home?

Exercise 7 Negative: 1 don't have 2 doesn't need 3 didn't use 4 don't have 5 doesn't do 6 doesn't need 7 didn't have 8 didn't
have 9 didn't need 10 doesn't do 11 doesn't have 12 didn't have
13 doesn't do 14 doesn't have 15 don't have 16 didn't dare
17 didn't do 18 doesn't have 19 doesn't dare 20 didn't have
21 didn't do 22 doesn't need 23 didn't have 24 didn't have
25 didn't use 26 don't do 27 didn't have 28 didn't dare

Interrogative: 1 do they have 2 does he need 3 did he use 4 do
they have 5 does she do 6 does he need 7 did he have 8 did she
have 9 did her hair need 10 does he do 11 does she have 12 did
she have 13 does he do 14 does he have 15 do the children have
16 did she dare 17 did you do 18 does he have 19 does he dare
20 did they have 21 did the drink 22 does my watch need 23 did
he have 24 did you have 25 did she use 26 do you do 27 did he
have 28 did he dare

Exercise 8 1 wasn't 2 didn't 3 couldn't 4 had to 5 wouldn't
6 could 7 wasn't 8 wasn't 9 didn't need to 10 hoped that Tom
would 11 did 12 said that Ann might 13 was 14 did 15 did . . .

could 16 could 17 had to 18 dared 19 didn't 20 had 21 were
22 Had you to/Did you have to 23 didn't need to 24 hoped, he'd
25 might 26 Did you understand . . . he was saying? I didn't
27 were 28 might 29 didn't 30 weren't, were 31 thought, might
32 wanted . . . if she could 33 couldn't 34 was, would 35 could,
couldn't 36 didn't, would.

Exercise 9 (Affirmative answers all begin with **Yes** + the first of the
answers given. Negative answers all begin with **No** + the second of
the answers given.)

1 Yes, it is. No, it isn't. 2 I do/don't 3 I can/can't 4 he
does/doesn't 5 it is/isn't 6 I am/I'm not 7 I must/needn't 8 we
are/aren't 9 he did/didn't 10 it would/wouldn't 11 you
may/mayn't 12 it is/isn't 13 she will/won't 14 I do/don't 15 you
should/shouldn't 16 I can/can't 17 I am/I'm not 18 they
could/couldn't 19 it is/isn't 20 they were/weren't 21 she
will/won't 22 you ought/oughtn't 23 you should/shouldn't 24 he
was/wasn't 25 I have/haven't 26 we must/needn't 27 he did/didn't
28 I would/wouldn't 29 it is/isn't 30 I do/don't 31 you can/can't
32 I will/won't 33 I am/I'm not 34 you are/aren't 35 you
must/needn't 36 it was/wasn't

Exercise 10 Part 1 The answers in this section all begin with **So**.
1 So has John. 2 . . . is she. 3 . . . can his wife. 4 . . . ought you.
5 . . . should you. 6 . . .will Tom. 7 . . . was the second. 8 . . . did
my brother. 9 . . . must your son. 10 . . . does that. 11 . . . is my
friend. 12 . . . did I.

Part 2 The answers in this section all begin with **Neither/Nor**.
13 Neither/Nor has Tom. 14 . . . should Tom. 15 . . . must I.
16 . . . can his sister. 17 . . . does Ann. 18 . . . could Andrew.
19 . . . are you. 20 . . .does that. 21 . . . will mine. 22 . . . had the
taxi-driver. 23 . . . did anyone else. 24 . . . would my mother.

Part 3 The answers in this section all begin with **But**. 25 But Mary
wasn't. 26 . . . she was. 27 . . . your brother needn't. 28 . . . I
can't. 29 . . . James did. 30 . . . Stanley must. 31 . . . a dog
would. 32 . . . his wife won't. 33 . . . my neighbour has. 34 . . .
that beach isn't. 35 . . . you needn't. 36 . . . I do.

Exercise 11 Part 1 1 Yes, we must. 2 Yes, you were. 3 Yes, she
does. 4 Yes, she may. 5 Yes, he could. 6 (Oh), so there is! 7 Yes,
he does. 8 (Oh), so it is! 9 Yes, it was. 10 Yes, it might. 11 Yes,
they did. 12 Yes, it is.

Part 2 All answers begin with **No.** 13 No, they don't. 14 . . . he
didn't. 15 . . . it isn't. 16 . . . he can't. 17 . . . it wasn't. 18 . . . it
wouldn't. 19 . . . it hasn't. 20 . . . they don't. 21 . . . they didn't.
22 . . . it hasn't. 23 . . . you don't. 24 . . . he mightn't.

Part 3   25 No, I'm not.   26 Yes, you did.   27 (Oh) yes, they were!
28 (Oh) yes, you were!   29 No, she wouldn't.   30 No, I didn't.
31 No, you can't.   32 No, it doesn't.   33 (Oh) yes, he did!   34 (Oh) no,
they don't.   35 No, they shouldn't.   36 No, she didn't.

Exercise 12   1 are you   2 is she   3 do you   4 did he   5 is it   6 was
she   7 has he   8 will you   9 did I   10 does he   11 do you   12 does it
13 should they 14 are you   15 could they   16 do you   17 was there
18 need I   19 was it   20 did you   21 will it   22 does she   23 did it
24 should he   25 could she   26 are you   27 would you   28 had he
29 were they   30 would you   31 does he   32 has he   33 could he
34 need I   35 were there   36 was it

Exercise 13   1 can't they   2 isn't he   3 didn't he   4 haven't they
5 wasn't he   6 shouldn't he   7 couldn't it   8 isn't he   9 isn't it
10 can't he   11 won't it   12 doesn't she   13 hasn't she   14 didn't
they 15 doesn't she   16 doesn't he   17 didn't he   18 don't they
19 haven't I   20 hasn't he   21 isn't she   22 didn't they   23 mightn't
he 24 mustn't we   25 hadn't you   26 wouldn't you   27 don't they
28 oughtn't she   29 wasn't it   30 don't they   31 won't you   32 didn't
he 33 won't there   34 hadn't you   35 wouldn't you   36 couldn't you

Exercise 14   1 don't you   2 do you   3 is it   4 does it   5 wasn't it
6 was there   7 didn't they   8 wasn't there   9 did they   10 does she
11 doesn't she   12 wouldn't she   13 didn't he   14 did he   15 wasn't
she 16 oughtn't he   17 did they   18 do they   19 can't they   20 does
he 21 is it   22 did it   23 aren't they   24 hadn't we   25 wouldn't it
26 would it   27 isn't it   28 wouldn't she   29 shouldn't they
30 weren't they   31 didn't she   32 does he   33 didn't there   34 is
there   35 will he   36 does it

Exercise 15   1 –   2 to   3 to   4 to   5 –   6 to   7 to   8 –   9 –   10 to
11 to 12 to   13 (to)   14 –   15 –   16 –, to   17 to   18 to   19 –   20 –
21 to   22 to 23 –   24 to   25 –   26 to   27 –, (to)   28 –   29 –   30 to
31 –   32 to   33 to 34 –   35 to   36 –

Exercise 16   I can/could   2 be able   3 had   4 had   5 must, needn't
6 didn't dare   7 ought/will have   8 used   9 is to be   10 could
11 shall   12 would, might   13 would   14 had   15 don't have/need
16 was to have   17 should/ought to   18 might/should   19 will have
20 used, would   21 should   22 will   23 must have   24 may   25 were
26 have   27 oughtn't   28 might

Exercise 17   (As mentioned in the note, the **do/did** form could be
used throughout except in no. 27, and of course for the future.)

1 hasn't even (got)   2 has (got), has/has always got   3 don't have,
have (got) 4 has (got)   5 haven't you (got)   6 did you have/had you

Key

7 has the alphabet (got)   8 do the houses have/have the houses (got)
9 have you (got), haven't (got)   10 do you ever have   11 he'll have
12 don't usually have   13 have you (got)   14 don't always have
15 hasn't your door (got)   16 have you (got), have   17 haven't (got)
18 has (got)   19 have you   20 has this desk (got), don't ever
have/never have   21 do you ever have   22 do babies have   23 has/has
a pentagon got   24 has, does she have   25 have, won't/don't have
26 do you have   27 have you (got), have (got)   28 have you (got), I
only have/have only (got), will have   29 have you (got)   30 have you
(got), have, haven't (got)   31 hasn't he (got)   32 have, didn't
have/hadn't   33 didn't you have   34 do red-haired people always
have/have red-haired people always got   35 hasn't (got)   36 have you
(got)

Exercise 18   1 are having   2 did you have/had you   3 is having
4 are having   5 does he have, he usually has   6 do you have   7 do
you have, have   8 do you have, have   9 don't you have   10 were
having   11 did you have/had you 12 are having   13 will you have
14 are having   15 had   16 did you have   17 am having   18 are
having   19 was having   20 do English people always have   21 don't
have/haven't   22 are having   23 don't have   24 did you have/had you
had   25 did you have/had you   26 am having   27 does he have
28 did you have/had you   29 had   30 are having   31 didn't
have/hadn't   32 are having   33 am having   34 is having   35 does he
ever have   36 had, did you have/had you

Exercise 19   1 am having   2 will have   3 had   4 am having   5 have
just had   6 am having   7 did you have   8 does he have   9 do you
have   10 don't you have   11 do you have   12 am having   13 have it
x-rayed   14 have it repaired   15 have them shortened   16 am having
them typed   17 have it tuned   18 have the document photocopied
19 had them dyed   20 have it mended   21 have it set   22 have just
had it re-charged   23 to have it enlarged   24 have just had them
sharpened   25 have my car serviced   26 have it seen to   27 had my
watch cleaned   28 is having her portrait painted   29 they had the
man arrested   30 he had the car towed   31 are having a garage built
32 have my windows cleaned   33 had my eyes tested   34 is having
his fortune told   35 had the oysters opened   36 had my ears pierced

Exercise 20   1 is being/will be ruined   2 is to make/is making
3 were   4 being, being   5 were to be/should be extinguished   6 have
you been   7 is being pulled down   8 was to put   9 isn't it   10 are to
stay   11 should be asked   12 were   13 I am to go   14 is being
carried   15 to be   16 were   17 were to have taken   18 is being
taught   19 was, will be, were   20 to be   21 was to have
been   22 should be sent   23 will there be   24 had been   25 is to
open/is opening   26 were being taken   27 was to have been
28 would you be   29 is to be/is being/will be   30 was to have run

31 was still being painted   32 should be printed   33 are being/have been translated   34 were   35 was to do   36 is to be

Exercise 21   (Affirmatives are not given in their contracted form but would normally be contracted in speech.)

1 It is, It is   2 is it, It is   3 It was, there were   4 It is, There will be 5 it was 6 It is, it is   7 There are, there is   8 There is; It will be, it is, it is, there will be   9 There is, it is   10 It was, it was   11 There was; There were   12 There was; There were   13 It is, it is   14 It is; There are   15 It is; It is   16 It will be; there will   17 There is; Is it 18 There are, it is   19 It is   20 it was   21 there are; there is; It is 22 It is, it is   23 There is, there are; It is *or* There was, there were; It was   24 Is there; it is; there is/there will be   25 there was; there was 26 There was; It was, there was   27 There are; There is, it is, isn't it   28 It is; there is; There is, there is/will be   29 There are; It is, there is   30 It is; It is; It is   31 there is; it was, wasn't it   32 it was/would be   33 It was; it was, there was   34 Is there; there is; is it   35 There is   36 It is; There is

Exercise 22   1 can, could, can't/couldn't   2 will be able to   3 won't be able to   4 can't . . . can't *or* couldn't . . . couldn't   5 shall/will be able to   6 will never be able to   7 couldn't, can't   8 will you be able to   9 won't be able to   10 could, couldn't   11 can, can, can't 12 can't, can't/couldn't, can't/couldn't   13 could/was able to   14 was able to   15 could/was able to, couldn't/wasn't able to   16 were able to   17 were you able to/could you   18 couldn't/wasn't able to   19 was able to   20 were able to   21 could/was able to   22 was able to 23 was able to   24 was able to   25 could/can, could   26 could, couldn't   27 could, couldn't, can't   28 could   29 couldn't/wouldn't be able to   30 couldn't/wouldn't be able to   31 could/can, can't 32 could, could   33 could/can, couldn't/can't   34 couldn't/wouldn't be able to   35 couldn't/wasn't able to, couldn't/wasn't able to   36 could

Exercise 23   1 may   2 might   3 may/might   4 may/might   5 might 6 may   7 may   8 might   9 may   10 was allowed to   11 might 12 may   13 may/might   14 may/might, may/might   15 might 16 may   17 may   18 may   19 may/might   20 might   21 might 22 may/might   23 may/might   24 may   25 might   26 may/might 27 might/may   28 may/might   29 may 30 might   31 might 32 may/might   33 may   34 might   35 may/might   36 hasn't been allowed to

Exercise 24   1 has to   2 must   3 has to   4 have to   5 must   6 have to   7 had to   8 has to   9 had to   10 have to   11 must   12 will have to/have to   13 must   14 has to   15 must   16 have to   17 have to 18 must   19 must   20 have to   21 had to   22 must   23 have to 24 must   25 has to   26 must   27 will have to   28 must   29 had to

Key

30 have to   31 will have to   32 had to   33 have to   34 must/will have
to   35 must   36 have to

Exercise 25   (Add **not** to each of the following verbs.)

1 need   2 must   3 must   4 need   5 must   6 must   7 need   8 must
9 need   10 need   11 need   12 must   13 need   14 must   15 must
16 need   17 must 18 must   19 need   20 need   21 must   22 must
23 need   24 must   25 must 26 must   27 need   28 need   29 need
30 need   31 need   32 must   33 need   34 must   35 must   36 need

Exercise 26   (**didn't have to** is replaceable by **didn't need to**.)

1 he doesn't have/hasn't (got) to   2 did you have to   3 I don't have
to   4 they will have to   5 we didn't have to   6 we didn't have to
7 you needn't come   8 I never have to   9 shan't/won't have to
10 you needn't   11 shall we have to   12 you don't have to   13 I didn't
have to   14 we don't have to   15 have you got to/must you/need you
16 do people have to   17 shall I have to   18 don't have to   19 we
didn't have to   20 you needn't   21 we didn't have to   22 do we have
to/must we   23 did you have to   24 I didn't have to   25 you won't
have to   26 they didn't have to   27 do you have to/have you got to
28 did you have to/had you to   29 didn't have to   30 shall I have to
31 do you have to/have you got to   32 I didn't have to   33 do French
children have to   34 did you have to   35 I didn't have to   36 did you
have to

Exercise 27   1 must have been   2 can't/couldn't have been
3 needn't have helped   4 must have left   5 can't/couldn't have
escaped   6 needn't have given   7 can't/couldn't have seen   8 must
have started   9 can't have been   10 needn't have bought   11 must
have been   12 must have borrowed   13 must have stolen   14 needn't
have done   15 needn't have said   16 can't/couldn't have understood
17 can't/couldn't have done   18 must have been   19 can't/couldn't
have walked   20 can't have been   21 must have been
22 can't/couldn't have had   23 needn't have watered   24 must have
taken   25 can't/couldn't have been   26 can't/couldn't have watered
27 must have been   28 needn't have sent   29 needn't have made
30 must have been   31 must have been   32 can't/couldn't have seen
33 can't/couldn't have come   34 needn't have lent   35 needn't have
spoken   36 must have fallen

3 Present and past tenses

Exercise 28   1 wishes   2 passes   3 helps   4 changes   5 watches
6 worries   7 cashes   8 carries   9 washes   10 goes   11 lays
12 bounces   13 astonishes   14 does he like   15 costs   16 fishes

17 forgets 18 catches 19 misses 20 mixes 21 freezes 22 flies
23 matches 24 realizes 25 uses 26 does he do, does, lies
27 hurries 28 pushes 29 kisses 30 boxes 31 dresses 32 relies
33 snatches 34 fries 35 rises 36 does

Exercise 29 Negative: 1 don't know 2 doesn't have 3 doesn't love
4 don't wear 5 doesn't trust 6 doesn't try 7 doesn't close
8 doesn't miss 9 don't like 10 doesn't finish 11 doesn't live
12 doesn't bully 13 doesn't heat 14 doesn't have 15 doesn't carry
16 doesn't believe 17 doesn't dance 18 don't remember 19 doesn't
play 20 doesn't worry 21 don't work 22 doesn't leave 23 doesn't
arrange 24 doesn't agree 25 don't bark 26 don't complain
27 doesn't enjoy 28 doesn't engage 29 doesn't look 30 don't sell
31 doesn't charge 32 doesn't cut 33 don't pick 34 doesn't leave
35 doesn't relax 36 doesn't refuse

Interrogative: 1 do you know 2 does he have 3 does he love 4 do
they wear 5 does he trust 6 does he try 7 does the park close
8 does he miss 9 do the children like 10 does he finish 11 does he
live 12 does he bully 13 does it heat 14 does she have 15 does she
carry 16 does he believe 17 does she dance 18 do you remember
19 does she play 20 does he worry 21 do these thieves usually
work 22 does he leave 23 does Ann arrange 24 does she agree
25 do their dogs bark 26 do their neighbours often complain
27 does Tom enjoy 28 does he engage 29 does Tom look 30 do
they sell 31 does he charge 32 does she cut 33 do they pick
34 does the last train leave 35 does he relax 36 does she refuse

Exercise 30 1 isn't working, is swimming 2 is teaching 3 isn't Ann
wearing 4 is flying 5 is Tom doing, is cleaning 6 is going, is
someone bringing 7 is it raining, is raining 8 are you mending
9 aren't telling, am not telling 10 is moving, is painting 11 is
sweeping 12 are you reading, am reading 13 is shining, are singing
14 is knocking, am just coming, am just washing 15 is always ringing
up and asking 16 are you making, is someone coming 17 is lying
18 are you using 19 are you doing, am going 20 are having, is
catching 21 am doing 22 are you typing, you are making 23 is
resting 24 are digging, are they doing, are looking 25 is making, are
repairing 26 are doing, are cutting 27 are you waiting, am waiting,
is just getting 28 are saying, is making 29 is always losing . . . and
asking 30 are you looking . . . is something happening
31 am bathing 32 are rushing, are jumping out and unrolling 33 is
pouring, are stopping, is trying 34 is climbing, is helping, are
sliding 35 is waving, is going 36 is coming, is carrying, is/are
cheering

Exercise 31 1 don't build, use 2 is having 3 drinks, is drinking
4 does she do, plays, watches 5 is raining, haven't 6 leaves

Key

7 speaks, don't understand 8 is making, makes 9 wears 10 don't
like 11 am wearing 12 is reading 13 am redecorating 14 is
boiling 15 are you enjoying, am enjoying, want 16 do you get, go,
am going 17 are you putting, am going, are you coming, do you
mind 18 do you owe, I owe, do you intend 19 do you belong, do you
read, do you change, I change 20 learns, doesn't seem
21 always buy/am always buying, win 22 do you like, am giving
23 promise, promise 24 do you always write 25 do you love, like,
don't love 26 do you dream, dream, eat, have 27 smells, do you
keep 28 are always complaining/always complain 29 are using
30 is always saying/always says, does 31 do you know, falls 32 are
you writing, write, do you want 33 are having, wonder, are talking
34 do you believe, don't believe, do you read 35 is making, do you
think, doesn't matter, makes 36 is smoking, expect, are building,
does, doesn't seem, don't you put

Exercise 32 1 does Tom think, thinks, agree 2 does this one cost, i
costs 3 do you hear, is blowing 4 do you see, am looking, don't see
5 listens, is always thinking 6 deserts, goes 7 do you understand,
don't understand 8 do you have, eat, drink 9 rises, see, are
picketing 10 are you walking, walk, am hurrying, am meeting,
doesn't like 11 wish, keeps, think, wants 12 do you recognize,
think, don't remember 13 wonder, waiting for 14 is waiting, want
15 don't you see, see, am not wearing, does it say, says 16 is always
borrowing/always borrows, remembers 17 do you need, do you feel
18 does it save, take, doesn't matter 19 am saving, am going
20 think, are getting 21 are looking, is just taking 22 does, is
always working 23 is he doing, think, is polishing 24 is coming, do
you want 25 is Peter getting on, seems 26 is Mrs Pitt looking/does
Mrs Pitt look, is smoking, and (is) dropping 27 leave, arrive, spend,
set, sounds, get 28 makes, finds, goes, does not forget, returns,
looks 29 finds, recognizes, coils, kills 30 does the snake feel, don't
know, ends 31 do you end, begins, put, prefers 32 does the word
'catastrophe' mean, means 33 are you waiting, am waiting, doesn't
open, know, want, starts/is starting 34 are you smoking, don't
smoke, am smoking, want, says, removes 35 owns, don't know, uses
knows, owns 36 do you mind, ask, depends, concerns, refuse

Exercise 33 1 went 2 met 3 wore 4 made 5 got 6 understood
7 shut 8 spoke 9 left 10 read 11 ate 12 saw 13 sang 14 cried,
was 15 knew 16 thought I knew 17 rose 18 took 19 bought
20 dreamt 21 laid 22 felt 23 knew, wanted 24 paid 25 bit
26 smelt 27 cost 28 hurt 29 lay 30 drank 31 grew 32 rode
33 fell 34 fought, met 35 put 36 slept

Exercise 34 Negative: the answer in each case is **did not/didn't** +
infinitive, e.g. 1 did not/didn't see

Interrogative: the answer in each case is **did** + subject + infinitive, e.g. 1 did she see

The infinitives are as follows: 1 see 2 hear 3 sleep 4 look
5 drink 6 set 7 think 8 catch 9 hide 10 find 11 bleed 12 choose
13 lend 14 teach 15 hurt 16 break 17 come 18 lose 19 write
20 fly 21 draw 22 lay 23 fall 24 lose 25 forbid 26 send
27 keep 28 ride 29 spend 30 sell 31 ring 32 rise 33 run
34 shake 35 forgive 36 broadcast

Exercise 35 1 were doing, was playing, was listening 2 was
getting 3 were rushing 4 was travelling 5 was wearing 6 was
redecorating 7 were working 8 was running 9 were playing, were
leaning 10 was working, was shopping 11 was sailing 12 were
going 13 were talking 14 was studying 15 was cooking 16 was
dieting, was trying 17 were you talking, was talking 18 was
climbing 19 was working 20 were bathing, were looking, were
playing 21 was he living 22 was standing, was waiting 23 was
practising 24 were carrying 25 were fighting, was trying, were they
fighting 26 was sitting, was reading 27 were doing, was weeding,
was cutting 28 were mending 29 was/were clapping 30 was
making, was saying 31 was learning 32 was repairing 33 was
always trying 34 were fishing 35 were writing 36 was wandering

Exercise 36 1 was burning 2 was writing 3 was making 4 left
5 was just leaving 6 was watching, turned, went 7 stood 8 was
playing, insisted 9 was walking 10 was having, lunched 11 wore,
carried 12 did you think, liked 13 shared, was always
complaining/always complained 14 realized, was travelling 15 was
playing, threw 16 was just opening, blew 17 was opening, heard,
put, crawled 18 was looking, found 19 saw, were you doing
20 were playing, heard, hid, took 21 was cleaning, went, killed
22 didn't allow, was blowing 23 was crossing/crossed, stepped, fell
24 was still lying, saw 25 saw, stopped 26 did you damage, ran,
were driving, were going 27 was getting/got, started, fell 28 called,
was already getting up 29 was mending/mended, got 30 heard,
went, opened, didn't recognize, wasn't wearing 31 were sitting, was
doing, was knitting, were reading, smiled, said 32 were dancing,
broke, stole 33 knew, were looking, hid, went 34 was always
buying 35 told, was spending/spent, listened 36 began, banged

Exercise 37 1 woke, was always getting/always got, went, bought
2 had to, usually grazed/was usually grazing 3 didn't normally chase,
made, was crossing, went 4 annoyed, began 5 was carrying, was
raining, threw, ran 6 stopped, began, was doing 7 awoke, was
sitting, was looking, called, turned, smiled 8 did you interrupt, was
having 9 was carrying, heard 10 was looking, noticed 11 were
walking/walked, heard, turned, held, stopped 12 arrived, was

Key

waiting, was wearing, (was) looking/looked, saw, waved, shouted, was
saying/said, was making 13 escaped, was working, was wearing
14 was travelling, began 15 didn't like, was trying 16 was making,
felt, brought, was able 17 saw, was painting, did you like, was only
just starting, saw 18 took, was being, were still listening, left/were
leaving 19 was, had to, was enjoying 20 were coming, stopped,
said, was looking, asked 21 saw, were you using, was using, were
you riding 22 was knitting 23 was, said, hoped, was enjoying
24 was watering, began, put, went 25 was just writing, remembered,
had 26 found, was digging, belonged 27 saw, was hurrying, asked,
was going, said, was speaking, wasn't 28 called, was still working
29 came, was smoking, had, threw, hoped 30 noticed, was rising,
were you smoking, came, asked 31 was swimming, stole, had to
32 said, were working, wanted 33 said, was building, thought
34 woke, said, thought, was trying 35 did you lend, was still reading,
didn't know, were still reading 36 came, woke, started, woke, came,
said, said, didn't hear, was barking, went, telephoned

Exercise 38 1 Have you been, I've been 2 have you had, have
3 has the post come, has 4 have you seen, haven't 5 has someone
wound, has 6 haven't finished 7 has just gone 8 has taken 9 has
stopped 10 have you heard, haven't 11 have just washed 12 has
stolen 13 have you explained, have 14 have gone 15 have you had,
have had 16 has Charles passed, has 17 has the milkman left, has
left 18 have lived 19 have you known, have known 20 have just
made 21 has Mary watered, has 22 haven't you made, haven't
23 haven't you mended, haven't had 24 have you dived, haven't
25 have you ever left, haven't 26 have asked 27 has always
refused 28 have you ever ridden 29 have bought 30 has he posted
31 hasn't he finished, has had 32 have often seen, have never
spoken 33 have you ever eaten, haven't 34 have just heard
35 have recaptured 36 haven't paid

Exercise 39 1 have, wound 2 haven't, ate 3 has, fed 4 haven't,
have only repaired 5 have done, did 6 haven't, haven't found
7 have, made 8 haven't, have been 9 haven't, haven't seen
10 have, went 11 have driven, drove 12 hasn't, has, went 13 have,
was 14 has, spoke 15 have only spent, have 16 haven't saved,
have saved 17 hasn't, went 18 haven't seen, saw, didn't see
19 have, paid 20 haven't, flew 21 bit, has bitten 22 planted,
haven't 23 has, wrote 24 haven't, drank, haven't drunk

Exercise 40 1 have you lived/have you been living, have lived/have
been living 2 lived, went 3 did you wear, insisted 4 left, cut, have
worn 5 wrote 6 has written, has just finished 7 flew, did you see
8 haven't seen 9 hasn't smoked 10 composed 11 did he arrive,
arrived 12 did you lock 13 read, enjoyed 14 haven't finished
15 have never drunk 16 have written 17 has stopped 18 have just

cleaned 19 left, got 20 did, was 21 has just gone 22 went
23 have you had, had 24 met 25 did you see 26 began, lasted,
enjoyed 27 has just begun 28 has the newspaper come 29 arrived,
started 30 has been 31 wrote 32 have missed 33 broke 34 has
been 35 worked, retired, went 36 have you been, spent, did you
have, stopped

Exercise 41 1 haven't seen, told 2 bought, did you pay, paid 3 did
you find, found, didn't you leave 4 have lost, have you seen, haven't,
did you last wear, wore, left 5 has just left, has been, has never
bought 6 left, did he go, didn't see, went 7 served, did that war
begin, began, lasted 8 did you vote, voted, wasn't, was, lost 9 did
you like, liked, quarrelled, dismissed, were, was 10 didn't know,
knew, have you known, have known 11 hasn't had, have been
12 did you hear, did, did you think 13 didn't know, were, have you
been, have been, have you been, went 14 have you tried, tried,
found, started 15 have you seen, has anything happened, have
escaped 16 has Mary fed, fed, did she give, gave 17 have you
known, have known, did he do, came, was 18 have you seen, hasn't
been bought 19 has the plumber been, stayed, did he do, turned,
emptied 20 have you been, have been, did you enjoy, took, did you
win, came 21 has that been, has been, have written, has been
22 have just been, have you seen, haven't, haven't read, read, was,
did Tolstoy write, wrote, did he write 23 brought, did he do,
wanted 24 have you been, have been, did he take, did, did it hurt
25 said, hasn't phoned 26 have just received, haven't paid, didn't I
give, did, spent/have spent 27 have you been, have just started, did
you find, answered 28 have you finished, have done 29 have cut,
did it happen, slipped 30 did you get, got 31 did you meet, did,
had 32 lost, has been, did he lose, was 33 has been, did you see,
happened, ran 34 phoned, got 35 did not wear, have worn 36 has
been, have just taken, has bought

Exercise 42 Affirmative: the answer in each case is **have/has** + **been**
+ present participle, e.g. 1 have been making

Negative: **have/has** + **not** + **been** + present participle, e.g.
16 haven't been eating

Interrogative: **have/has** + subject + **been** + present participle, e.g.
6 have you been doing

Present participles are as follows:
1 making 2 ringing 3 overworking 4 cutting 5 looking 6 doing,
working 7 studying 8 waiting 9 raining 10 arguing 11 bathing
12 driving 13 wearing 14 saying 15 trying 16 eating
17 speaking 18 flying 19 playing 20 shopping 21 living 22 eating
23 looking 24 leaking 25 digging, helping 26 asking 27 using

28 driving   29 going   30 snowing   31 crying, peeling   32 making
33 drinking   34 smoking   35 eating   36 trying

Exercise 43   1 have walked   2 have been walking/have walked
3 have been walking/have walked   4 have been making   5 have you
made, have made   6 has eaten   7 hasn't stopped   8 has been
drinking   9 have pulled   10 have been pulling   11 have you been
doing, have been picking   12 have you picked, have picked   13 have
slept   14 has been sleeping/has slept   15 has been riding   16 have
ridden   17 has been making   18 have been working/have worked
19 have heard   20 have been hearing/have heard   21 have been
greasing   22 have been polishing   23 have been working/have
worked, has never said   24 has been teaching/has taught   25 have
taught, have never met   26 have you been, have been pumping/have
pumped   27 have pumped   28 have been looking/have looked,
haven't found   29 has been coughing/has coughed   30 have you
heard, have known   31 have been trying, have said   32 has been
sounding   33 has been raining/has rained, has been postponed
34 has been hoping, hasn't dared   35 have been whispering, have you
been helping, has he been helping   36 have you been making, have
lost, have been trying, have been throwing

Exercise 44   1 for   2 for   3 since   4 for   5 for   6 since   7 since
8 since 9 for   10 since   11 for   12 for   13 for   14 for   15 since
16 since   17 for 18 since   19 for   20 since   21 since   22 since
23 for   24 since   25 since 26 since   27 for   28 since   29 since
30 for   31 for   32 since   33 for   34 for 35 for   36 since

4 Future forms

Exercise 45   1 are starting   2 is making   3 am taking   4 is calling
5 is playing   6 am meeting   7 are not starting   8 are you getting, am
going, is driving   9 is coming   10 are you giving, am giving   11 are
being   12 is coming   13 are having, are going   14 are you going, am
going   15 is not giving   16 am having   17 am buying   18 are being
19 am having   20 is/are meeting   21 are celebrating   22 am lending
23 are returning   24 are opening   25 are moving   26 am not taking
27 are getting   28 are you doing, am going   29 is flying   30 is
starting   31 is giving, are you going   32 is being, am meeting   33 am
catching, are you leaving, am not taking   34 is sending   35 am going,
is taking   36 am lending

Exercise 46   Affirmative: the answer in each case is **am/is/are** +
going to + infinitive, e.g. 1 are going to miss

Negative answers: **am/is/are** + **not** + **going to** + infinitive, e.g. 22 am
not going to do

Interrogative answers: **is/are** + subject + **going to** + infinitive, e.g.
3 are you going to pay

Exercise 47 (**be going to** is possible in all these sentences, but where
the present continuous tense is given in the key, that is the better one
to use.)

1 am playing 2 is having 3 am going to light 4 are having 5 is
being, are you putting, am putting 6 are you going, am going, am not
buying/am not going to buy 7 am not going to do 8 am having 9 is
coming, are you putting, am putting 10 is starting 11 am spending
12 is going to build 13 are you going to tell, am going to tell 14 is
starting 15 is opening 16 is speaking 17 is closing 18 are you
having, am having 19 am collecting 20 are taking 21 am giving
22 is singing 23 is going, is he flying, is going 24 is seeing 25 is he
going to wash 26 is ringing 27 is going to ask 28 are giving, are
inviting 29 is playing, is playing 30 are launching, are you coming
31 are you going to do 32 am picking 33 are you going, am going, is
calling 34 am competing 35 isn't coming 36 am going to read

Exercise 48 Affirmative answers: 1st person **will/shall** + infinitive,
2nd and 3rd person **will** + infinitive, e.g. 1 will/shall know

Negative answers: as above with **not**, e.g. 7 will not/won't catch

Interrogative answers: as above with **will/shall** + subject + infinitive,
e.g. 2 will you be

Exercise 49 (**shall** can be replaced by **will** in these answers.
Contractions may be used.)

1 shall recognize 2 will see/am seeing ('am seeing' implies a definite
arrangement) 3 is playing 4 is coming 5 am going 6 shall know
7 shall owe 8 shall believe 9 am having 10 will have 11 is
being/will be 12 is coming 13 is catching 14 are you meeting, am
meeting 15 are you riding/will you ride 16 will Mrs Pitt say, won't
mind 17 will it matter 18 won't forget 19 is leaving 20 shall
remember 21 will break 22 will never forgive 23 will like 24 are
laying 25 will see 26 will grow 27 will understand 28 will
scratch 29 shall be 30 won't pass 31 is going 32 am moving
33 will soon forget 34 will wait 35 won't write 36 will be

Exercise 50 (**shall** can be replaced by **will**. Contractions may be
used.)

1 will go 2 will telephone 3 will send 4 am going to learn 5 are
you going to do 6 will call, will translate 7 are you going to buy, am
not going to eat, am going to eat 8 are you going to redecorate 9 am
going to change, will help 10 are you going to put 11 am going to
put 12 are you going to do, am going to be 13 am going to shorten

14 won't lend 15 will cut 16 am going to attend 17 will ask 18 am
going to open 19 is going to take 20 will ask 21 am going to get
22 am going to develop 23 will make 24 are going to tow 25 am
going to give up/am giving up 26 will say 27 will lend 28 are going
to raffle 29 are going to clear 30 will mend 31 will give 32 am
going to make 33 am going to shorten 34 am going to buy 35 are
you going to do 36 am going to give

Exercise 51 1 will you open 2 are you going to do 3 are you going
to paint 4 will you read 5 are you going to eat 6 aren't you going
to climb 7 will you listen 8 will you put 9 will you have 10 are
you going to make 11 aren't you going to answer 12 will you come
13 are you really going to read 14 are you going to buy, will you
buy 15 will you lend, are you going to fish 16 are you going to
finish 17 will you give, are you going to make 18 are you going to
leave 19 are you going to bath, will you help 20 will you drive
21 are you going to ride 22 are you going to eat 23 will you have
24 are you really going to call 25 are you going to paint 26 will you
be ready 27 will you sit 28 will you do 29 will you be angry
30 are you going to work 31 will you call 32 are you going to walk
33 will you sign 34 are you going to give 35 are you going to
explore 36 will you cook

Exercise 52 Form of affirmative answer: **shall** or **will** ('ll) as
appropriate + **be** + present participle, e.g. I shall/will be sitting.
Negative answer: 19 won't be looking. Interrogative answers:
23 will the children be doing 26 will the tide be doing

Exercise 53 (**shall** can be replaced by **will** in these answers.
Contractions may be used.)

1 will be walking 2 will walk 3 shall be bathing 4 will wash
5 shall be doing 6 shall be working/am working 7 will have 8 will
be looking 9 shall be thinking/shall think 10 will assemble 11 will
meet, shall I recognize, will be wearing 12 will leave, shall be
going/am going 13 will be debating/are debating 14 will go 15 will
be working 16 will post, shall be going/am going 17 will be
dancing/will dance 18 will be letting off . . . and making/will let off
. . . and make 19 will remain 20 shall be sitting, won't be reading
21 will be going/will go 22 will be changing/will change 23 will
come 24 will bring 25 shall all be living 26 will be going/will go
27 shall not be playing 28 will be opening/will open 29 will drive
30 shall be entering 31 will hand 32 will be arriving/will arrive
33 will be leaving 34 will be using . . . and leaving/will use. . . and
leave 35 will bring, will catch 36 will put

Exercise 54 (In these answers **I/we won't** can be replaced by **I am
not going to/we are not going to** without any change in meaning. It is

also grammatically possible to replace **you/he/they won't** by the **going to** form, but this would make the negative much less emphatic. **shan't** is replaceable by **won't**.)

1 won't help 2 won't be meeting 3 won't cut 4 won't be cutting
5 won't be coming/isn't coming 6 won't come 7 won't lend 8 won't
be speaking/isn't speaking 9 won't work 10 shan't be working
11 won't have 12 shan't be teaching/am not teaching 13 won't
speak 14 shan't be writing 15 won't feed 16 won't go 17 won't
paint 18 shan't be taking 19 won't borrow 20 won't wash 21 shan't
be using 22 won't send 23 won't play 24 won't be singing/isn't
singing 25 won't play 26 won't be taking part/isn't taking part
27 won't eat 28 shan't be eating 29 won't ride 30 won't be
riding/isn't riding 31 won't give 32 won't be drinking 33 won't
open 34 won't tell 35 won't eat 36 won't be wearing

Exercise 55 1 are you going to feed 2 are you letting/are you going
to let/will you be letting 3 will you light 4 are you wearing/are you
going to wear/will you be wearing 5 will you wear 6 will you come
7 will you have 8 are you having/are you going to have 9 are you
going to study/will you be studying 10 will you be speaking 11 will
you turn 12 Any one of the four forms is possible here: 'Will you
take' implies that the matter has not yet been decided and that the
speaker is offering a choice of dates. The other forms would imply
that the matter has already been arranged and that the speaker is
merely asking for information. 13 will you be listening/are you going
to listen 14 will you help 15 will you be staying 16 will you lend
17 are you meeting/are you going to meet/will you be meeting
18 will you come 19 will you have 20 will you translate 21 will you
be using/are you using/are you going to use 22 will you be going/are
you going, will you get 23 will you come 24 will you be passing/are
you going to pass/are you passing, shall be spending/am going to
spend/am spending, will you get 25 are you going to keep 26 are
you travelling/are you going to travel 27 are you going to repair
28 will you hold 29 are you going/will you be going 30 will you
kindly explain 31 will you recognize 32 are you sending/are you
going to send 33 will you tell 34 are you going/will you be going
35 are you going to type/will you be typing 36 will you stop

Exercise 56 (**will** and **will not** may be contracted.)

1 shall/will 2 will 3 shall 4 shall 5 shall 6 shall 7 shall 8 will
9 shall 10 shall 11 shall 12 will 13 shall 14 shall 15 will
16 will 17 will 18 shall/will 19 will, will 20 shall 21 will
22 shall 23 will 24 shall 25 will, shall/will 26 will 27 shall, will
28 will 29 shall/will 30 shall/will 31 shall 32 won't, won't
33 will 34 shall 35 will, will 36 shall/will

Key

Exercise 57 (**will** and **shall** may be contracted.)

1 returns 2 are 3 strikes 4 hears 5 shall/will have 6 comes
7 turn 8 gets 9 won't start 10 goes 11 will see 12 will be
13 shall/will lend 14 will wake 15 will he ring 16 goes 17 is
18 shall/will give, comes 19 see 20 get 21 shall/will go 22 have
23 will fall 24 goes 25 arrives 26 lifts 27 will go on 28 will
become 29 won't move 30 will go on 31 learns 32 leap
33 shall/will have 34 get 35 begins 36 arrives

Exercise 58 Answers will all be: **have** + past participle of the verb
in brackets. **shall** can be used instead of **will** for the 1st person, e.g.
1 will/shall have taken. **will** can be contracted to 'll.

Exercise 59 (Contractions may be used.)

1 have taken 2 have finished/finish 3 have had 4 have been
5 goes/has gone 6 gets/has got 7 has done 8 have done 9 will see
10 have had 11 shall/will take 12 go 13 have seen 14 goes/has
gone 15 won't let 16 shall/will let 17 sees 18 won't hear 19 has
passed/passes 20 has sold 21 have swept/sweep 22 will get
23 will give 24 says 25 have returned/return 26 has been 27 have
signed 28 won't know 29 have subsided/subside 30 has left
31 shall/will have 32 have had 33 shall/will stay 34 have made
35 has eaten 36 will come/come

Exercise 60 (**should** is replaceable by **would** in nos. 6, 14, 26, 27,
30.)

1 would 2 would 3 should 4 would 5 would 6 should 7 should
8 would, would 9 should 10 would 11 should 12 would
13 would 14 should 15 should 16 would 17 should 18 would,
would 19 should 20 would 21 should 22 should 23 should
24 should 25 should 26 should 27 should 28 would 29 should
30 should/would, would 31 should 32 should, should 33 would
34 should 35 should 36 should

Exercise 61 1 should, should 2 would 3 should 4 should
5 would, would, would, would 6 should 7 should 8 would, would
9 should, should/would 10 should 11 would 12 would, should
13 should 14 should 15 should, would 16 should 17 should
18 would, should 19 should 20 would 21 should 22 would
23 should 24 should 25 would, would 26 would 27 should
28 would 29 should 30 should, should, would 31 should
32 should 33 should/would, would 34 would, would 35 should
36 would, would

5 Conditionals

Exercise 62 1 will give 2 stand 3 eats 4 will telephone 5 will arrest 6 reads 7 will steal 8 doesn't open 9 washes 10 needs 11 don't go 12 makes 13 is 14 hears 15 will make 16 will bury 17 won't be 18 doesn't start 19 won't let *or* don't let (habit) 20 goes 21 sells 22 will you repay 23 rises 24 works 25 turns/will turn 26 burns 27 don't like 28 will have 29 see 30 will you promise 31 don't believe 32 likes 33 will make 34 shan't/won't be able 35 knows 36 ring

Exercise 63 1 would type 2 knew 3 would look 4 played 5 wouldn't make 6 were 7 had 8 would you visit 9 gave 10 would buy 11 cleaned 12 would you be able 13 didn't belong 14 won 15 would you do 16 knew 17 gave 18 stopped 19 wouldn't come 20 saw 21 would/should be 22 would not be bitten 23 had 24 did 25 would grow 26 removed 27 would keep 28 lived 29 banned/were to ban 30 would offer 31 got 32 painted 33 changed 34 would you spend 35 had 36 wasn't

Exercise 64 (**should** in the following answers may be replaced by **would**; contractions may be used in the affirmative and negative.)

1 should have visited 2 would have won 3 had arrived 4 had been 5 should have been 6 had not seen 7 would have fallen 8 would you have accepted 9 had had 10 had known 11 should have offered 12 would not have stung 13 had realized 14 should have stopped 15 should have reached 16 should not have lent 17 had not sneezed 18 had put 19 would not have got 20 would not have tried 21 had spoken 22 would not have been 23 had known 24 had tried 25 would not have got 26 would not have put 27 had been 28 would have come 29 would not have turned 30 had looked 31 would have been captured 32 had tried 33 should have taken 34 would have saved 35 had not called 36 would not have burnt

Exercise 65 (In the affirmative and negative **shall** and **should** can be replaced by **will** and **would** respectively; and contractions may be used. **should** in sentences 1, 7, 11 however does not change.)

1 find/should find 2 shall have 3 will happen 4 had had 5 will you stay 6 would you choose 7 gets/should get 8 comes 9 will sit 10 didn't talk 11 shall/should I do 12 had read 13 had 14 shall go 15 would you do 16 run 17 will not be 18 comes 19 would not have 20 had worn 21 leaves 22 will fall 23 don't change 24 should not have bought 25 hung 26 would be able to/could 27 should have brought 28 would have been 29 would not have printed 30 should not buy 31 want 32 won't be 33 would jump 34 would answer 35 had made 36 had known

Key

Exercise 66 Open-ended sentences. No answers given.

Exercise 67 1 could I speak 2 speaking 3 could you come and do
4 couldn't 5 could come 6 could you come 7 could get, would
8 wouldn't, would, leave 9 thought you said 10 could get, couldn't
make 11 having, doesn't like 12 is always trying, cleaning,
thinks/says 13 does she want/would she like you to do 14 would
like/wants me to work 15 says/thinks it would be 16 worked, would
know 17 are you really thinking 18 like, like 19 would get
20 would Wednesday suit 21 would, to come 22 will, let 23 will,
won't 24 will, do

6 Infinitive

Exercise 68 1 do 2 sing 3 to swim 4 to live 5 to go, rain
6 say, understand 7 to see 8 repeat 9 use 10 ask, use 11 to
get, start 12 remember 13 to do 14 to go, wait 15 leave
16 open 17 (to) argue 18 to smoke 19 (to) move 20 play 21 to
accept 22 to arrive 23 know 24 wait 25 tell 26 send 27 go, to
meet 28 to have 29 leave, want, to take 30 to go, make, go
31 go, to visit 32 to know, to live 33 not to inform, (to) disobey
34 come, stay 35 take, make, drink 36 to disappoint, let, have

Exercise 69 1 to be 2 wish to make 3 want, to know
4 remember, look 5 to learn, to know 6 to be 7 not to feed
8 see, to speak 9 to travel, to arrive 10 know, to use, show 11 to
sign 12 open/opening, move/moving 13 to make, believe 14 to
have missed, go 15 shake/shaking 16 to try, to come 17 go,
promise, not to tell 18 like to come, walk 19 to ask, to tell, to get
20 to put, (to) keep 21 to read, answer 22 show, to open 23 say,
to say 24 to be 25 want, to tell, to call, to discuss 26 to give,
see/be seeing, not to forget 27 open/opening, throw/throwing 28 to
carry, help 29 to pick, to handle 30 crash/crashing,
burst/bursting 31 to do, wait, to let 32 crow/crowing 33 tell, be,
to check 34 come, go, be/have been 35 to learn 36 be, look `

Exercise 70 No answers given.

Exercise 71 1 too young to have 2 too cold to bathe 3 so kind as
to answer/kind enough to answer 4 too old to wear 5 long enough
to reach 6 enough money to live on 7 too furious to speak 8 hot
enough to boil 9 foolish enough to tell/so foolish as to tell 10 thin
enough to slip 11 too ill to eat 12 too wide to get through
13 strong enough to dance on 14 too terrified to move 15 big
enough to harm 16 strong enough to keep 17 too deep to wade
18 too lazy to get up 19 early enough to catch 20 so good as to

forward/good enough to forward 21 thick enough to walk on
22 too drunk to answer 23 too cold to have 24 rash enough to set
off/so rash as to set off 25 high enough to see 26 old enough to
understand 27 too snobbish to talk 28 too thick to push through
29 too mean to give 30 too impatient to listen 31 too tired to
walk 32 not dark enough to see 33 hot enough to fry 34 too bitter
to eat 35 so kind as to turn down/kind enough to turn down 36 too
selfish to put

Exercise 72 1 to leave 2 only to find 3 You are to go 4 so kind
as to lend/kind enough to lend 5 to mend/to be mended 6 to hear
7 for him to hear 8 It was stupid of me to be rude 9 to play with
10 for everyone to know 11 to sit 12 only to find 13 It was very
brave of him to rush 14 to wear 15 He is expected to broadcast
16 to cook in 17 only to learn 18 to open it with 19 seems to have
been committed 20 Is he likely to arrive 21 just about to leave
22 You are to be met 23 for them to have 24 He is said to have
been 25 to continue the strike 26 kind enough to translate/so kind
as to translate 27 for us to leave 28 It was stupid of you to sign
29 She is said to have 30 to swim 31 He is believed to be 32 He
appears to have been killed 33 to realize 34 The earth is said to
have been 35 only to discover 36 The murderer is said to be
hiding

Exercise 73 (**should** is replaceable by **ought to**.)

1 must have been 2 can't/couldn't have seen, must have dreamt
3 may/might have broken 4 needn't have carried 5 should have
gone 6 were to have been 7 can't/couldn't have been, must have
been 8 shouldn't have eaten 9 may/might not have understood
10 needn't have given 11 must have escaped 12 shouldn't have
lied 13 may/might have been, can't/couldn't have been 14 must
have cooked 15 needn't have brought 16 must have told 17 was
to have unveiled 18 may/might have been 19 must have met
20 should have done 21 can't/couldn't have caught 22 needn't
have opened 23 must have betrayed 24 shouldn't have driven
25 could have climbed 26 would have asked 27 should have been
abolished 28 shouldn't/needn't have boiled 29 was to have played
30 may/might have been 31 should have taken 32 must have had
33 may/might/could have fallen 34 must have been 35 needn't
have translated 36 shouldn't have looked

Exercise 74 (**I'd** is replaceable by **I should**. **should** (obligation) is
replaceable by **ought to** in nos. 5, 9, 13, 17. **may/might** in the
affirmative is normally replaceable by **could**.)

1 was to have married 2 needn't have repeated 3 seems to have
been 4 were to have set out 5 shouldn't have eaten, may/might
have been (**may** indicates that the danger is still present; **might** that

it is over). 6 must have worked 7 needn't have brought 8 I'd like to have bathed/I'd have liked to bathe/I'd have liked to have bathed 9 should have written 10 wouldn't have come 11 might/should have told, would have gone, wouldn't have liked 12 may/might have been, can't/couldn't have been 13 needn't/shouldn't have bought 14 can't/couldn't have been 15 seems to have enjoyed 16 must have been 17 should have stood 18 was to have gone 19 I'd like to have photographed/I'd have liked to photograph/I'd have liked to have photographed 20 must have been 21 may/might have been 22 can't/couldn't have been driving 23 must have taken 24 may/might not have 25 I'd like to have gone/I'd have liked to go/I'd have liked to have gone 26 can't/couldn't have seen 27 may have been 28 may/might have been started 29 must have had 30 may/might have read, can't/couldn't have read, must have told 31 may/might have been waiting 32 must have misheard 33 might have borrowed 34 I'd like to have asked/I'd have liked to ask/I'd have liked to have asked 35 must have been 36 is said to have been

7 Gerund, infinitive and participles

Exercise 75 1 gambling 2 making 3 arguing, working 4 watching, reading 5 making 6 crying 7 holding 8 speaking 9 driving 10 eating 11 putting 12 getting 13 breaking 14 reading 15 sliding 16 smoking 17 leaving, going 18 reading, smoking 19 losing 20 living, talking 21 buying 22 leaking 23 deciding 24 going 25 putting 26 being 27 working, finishing 28 making 29 working, going 30 writing 31 doing, doing 32 borrowing 33 being 34 talking, convincing 35 reading, thinking 36 listening, using

Exercise 76 1 seeing 2 having 3 to meet 4 to work 5 to see 6 waiting 7 not to touch 8 to lock, going 9 not to speak 10 behaving 11 to explain, to listen 12 smoking 13 to know 14 to disguise, dressing 15 to wait 16 showing, to work 17 walking, catch up 18 to understand 19 exceeding 20 playing, doing 21 to inform 22 overhearing 23 smoking, to smoke 24 going, saying 25 writing, waiting 26 to avoid being 27 giving, to speak 28 to persuade, to agree 29 cleaning, to be cleaned, to do 30 shutting, sitting 31 sneezing, sitting 32 talking, to finish 33 to give up jogging 34 stopping, forgetting to wind 35 realizing, helping 36 to make, rubbing

Exercise 77 1 answering, ring 2 letting, chase, being 3 driving, being driven 4 to start looking 5 lending, to cash 6 Lying, sitting 7 to go 8 neglecting to take 9 to show, to use 10 going, to see/seeing 11 telephoning, asking, to look 12 hearing, not to enter 13 to have, writing 14 to answer, replying 15 to explain, to

listen, grumbling 16 offering, to leave, (to) work 17 making, to
do 18 having to get up 19 to forget, worrying 20 remaining, to
help, to stay 21 to run, to have recovered 22 listening, hearing
23 to learn, reading, listening 24 to start, to wait 25 discussing,
having reached 26 having, to ride 27 (to) leave, meeting,
recognize 28 paying 29 to give 30 interrupting, repeating
31 cutting, to go 32 buying, selling 33 giving, to explain
34 asking, telling, to buy 35 to tell, looking 36 to be, to
erupt/erupting

Exercise 78 1 to ride, to do, coming, to come 2 spending, earning
3 being, to apologize 4 to eat 5 working, spending 6 looking,
being 7 posting 8 to lock, go, do 9 to learn, saying 10 trying to
interrupt, to wait, talking 11 doing, to move/moving 12 leaving, to
go 13 to drink 14 being, to wait 15 trying to make, adding
16 going, stay 17 to look, (to) take, looking, to do 18 getting up,
walking 19 listening, listening 20 to make/making, to see
21 doing 22 to put, to prevent, climbing 23 taking, to eat
24 ringing, asking, to do 25 waiting, to clear, to set 26 repeat, to
make, to do 27 leaving, sending, to tow 28 borrowing, asking, to
do 29 to offend, annoying 30 to be able to tell, gazing 31 getting,
to walk 32 to ask, to leave 33 setting, having been 34 to go
35 to go, (to) try to save, cutting 36 earn, scrubbing, make,
blackmailing

Exercise 79 1 beginning to slip/begin to slip/begin slipping, to save,
falling 2 falling, trying to keep 3 to lend, taking 4 to open
5 reading, to read 6 to book, to keep, to lose 7 to avoid being,
being/to be, waiting 8 to get, to ask 9 making, speak/speaking
10 to win, cheating 11 firing/to fire, graze 12 strike/striking, to
get 13 ringing/ring, to be coming to open 14 to go, to give 15 to
put, (to) watch, change/changing 16 to see, to avoid hitting 17 to
be, crackling 18 climbing, to explain, to say, to let, go
19 convincing, to get, leap 20 driving, doing, to do 21 to sit, (to)
hear, howling 22 getting, climbing, to do 23 roar/roaring, to
move/moving, waving 24 writing, to do, to go, see 25 walking, to
cross, thinking, to chase 26 to be having, thudding 27 getting, to
pay 28 to come, standing 29 to like making and flying . . . doing
30 to arrive, rising 31 sawing, fall/falling 32 to see/seeing,
crying/cry 33 jump/jumping, fall/falling 34 to wake, (to) hear,
beating 35 beginning to roll/begin to roll/begin rolling, to do, to
stop 36 laughing, slipping/slip

Exercise 80 1 Knowing that he was poor, I offered 2 Having
barricaded the windows, we assembled 3 Becoming tired of my
complaints, she turned it off 4 Finding/having found no one at
home, he left 5 Hoping to find the will, she searched 6 Having
removed all traces of his crime, he left 7 Realizing that he had

Key

missed the train, he began   8 Exhausted by his work, he threw
9 Having spent all his money, he decided   10 Having escaped from
prison, he looked   11 Having heard the story before, she didn't
want   12 Having found the money, they began   13 Entering the
room suddenly, she found   14 Turning on the light, I was
15 Having visited the museum, we decided   16 Thinking we were
lost, he offered   17 Having found his revolver and loaded it, he sat
18 Realizing that she couldn't move it alone, she asked   19 Having
fed the dog, he sat   20 Addressing the congregation, he said
21 Thinking he had made a mistake somewhere, he went
22 Looking/having looked through the fashion magazines, I realize
23 The tree, uprooted by the gale, had fallen   24 People sleeping in
the next room were   25 Knowing that the murderer was still at
large, I was   26 Having stolen the silver, he looked   27 Soaked to
the skin, we reached   28 Sitting/Seated in the front row, and using
. . . I saw   29 . . . sitting by the fire, you will take   30 Knowing that
. . . , I didn't like   31 Believing that she could trust him, she gave
32 Slates, ripped off by the gale, fell   33 The lion, finding his cage
door open and seeing no sign of his keeper, left   34 The
government, trying to tax people according to the size of their
houses, once put a tax   35 Having heard that the caves were
dangerous, I didn't like   36 Wearing extremely fashionable clothes
and surrounded by photographers and press men, she swept

Exercise 81   1 When leaving a car . . . you must leave the brakes
2 As/When I was wading etc *or* Wading across . . . I was swept off
my feet by   3 When a tank is being filled/When you are filling a
tank   4 Running into the room, she caught her foot on a rug and
fell   5 When I read the letter   6 When carrying . . . you should
never point it   7 When planting . . . you must take care   8 In his
first race, the horse he was riding fell   9 When paying by cheque,
you must show   10 Knowing me to be . . . , he was astonished to
hear that   11 As he believed that   12 As I passed/ *or* As/When I
was passing   13 When I am reading/When I read   14 As he left
15 I led the dog, barking furiously, out   16 After I had paid my
taxes, the amount   17 As I was writing   18 The boat, tied to a post,
was being tossed up and down by the sea   19 As the question had
been misunderstood, the wrong answer   20 We saw the first star,
shining in the sky   21 It is easy to have an accident when one is/you
are driving   22 The man saw a notice pinned to the door   23 They
read the words 'No Entry' written in   24 While he was cleaning his
gun it went off   25 When/As I was wondering where to go, an
advertisement   26 As I rushed out of the house, a lorry   27 As I sat
by the fire, it all comes back   28 We thought he would never
survive after falling from   29 When a fuse is being changed, the
electricity . . . *or* When you are changing a fuse you should switch
30 I saw a trailer with a boat on it being towed behind   31 As he
was sitting at the foot . . . a stone fell   32 The road was blocked by

170

a huge tree (which had been) uprooted 33 When he drove to work the traffic jams infuriated him 34 As I sat in the dentist's chair an idea 35 I felt sure that . . . would kill him, weakened as he was by his last illness 36 A scorpion bit him as he got out of bed

8 Passive

Exercise 82 1 wine should be opened . . . before it is used 2 steps had been cut 3 my shoes had been cleaned and my suit brushed 4 room is used 5 nails must not be hammered 6 pigs are used 7 a light was switched on and the door opened 8 picture had been slashed 9 theatre is being pulled down 10 wasn't the roof mended 11 All the shop windows were broken 12 system was being started because books were not being returned 13 each of us was asked 14 refreshments will be served 15 bicycles must not be left 16 books may be kept . . . they must be returned 17 hole had been cut 18 it is being delivered 19 he has already been told 20 bells were rung 21 nothing can be done unless we are given more 22 far more is being spent on food now than was spent 23 paintings will be exhibited 24 nothing more will be said . . . if the . . . gun is returned 25 he was told 26 My dog was stolen and brought back only when a £20 reward was offered. 27 he was given two weeks 28 flowers are made

Exercise 83 1 seals are fed 2 who was it written by? 3 compare clothes washed by us with clothes washed by any other 4 he expected to be offered 5 she was shown 6 oak was struck by lightning 7 it couldn't have been painted by T. because that kind of dress wasn't worn 8 she was stung by a jellyfish 9 special edition for . . . has been written 10 herbs used to be carried by judges 11 what was it written with? It was written with 12 shot was succeeded by an uneasy silence 13 were you interested by the idea? 14 he was given details 15 dams are made by beavers 16 engines used to be started by hand, now they are started by electricity 17 this was opposed by most people 18 a lot of the work is being done by students 19 dock was to have been opened by the PM 20 They recommend that new factories should be opened 21 a lot of men will be made redundant by the closure 22 instructions could be understood by anyone 23 children . . . will not be admitted 24 ship is to be manned by boys 25 camp was flooded by a rainstorm 26 He was kept awake all night by the howling 27 They suggested that the tests should be made 28 All this damage couldn't have been done by children

Exercise 84 1 why don't you get an oculist to test your eyes? 2 the authorities are to introduce this . . . limit 3 they are lengthening the runways 4 nurses are wakening patients 5 people say that B.

lived 6 British fishermen must offer any sturgeon that they catch to
the Queen 7 someone has altered this notice 8 squatters have been
using their houseboat 9 they were towing the . . . ship 10 get a
builder to put in a lift 11 The firm made a profit . . . but a loss of
. . . which they made . . . cancelled this 12 guests will wear evening
dress 13 the authorities put the ship . . . and forbade passengers
and crew 14 we shall have to find someone 15 They made him
surrender his passport 16 our opponents must have started 17 the
New Arts Gallery is to exhibit my paintings 18 experts have proved
that this scientific theory is false 19 they are to salvage the car
which the wind blew 20 police are guarding the house where they
found the dead man to prevent anyone from entering it and
interfering with the evidence 21 why didn't you either lock the car
or put it 22 people are saying that the government is spending too
little money 23 you could put your money to good use instead of
leaving it idle 24 people believed that the earth was flat 25 no one
has read this copy; no one has cut the pages 26 the police led away
the student who threw the stones 27 people say that early Egyptian
and Greek sailors used carrier pigeons 28 a strong police guard was
escorting the referee

9 Indirect speech

Exercise 85 (In many of these examples other pronouns would be
equally correct.)

1 told her I had . . . to show her 2 said nothing grew in her garden
. . . it never got 3 told his mother he was going away the next day
4 said he had been . . . he hadn't had 5 remarked that it wasn't so
foggy that day as it had been the day before 6 said that the
underpass was being opened two days later 7 said they had moved
into their flat but they didn't like it . . . their last one 8 said they
had . . . it didn't work 9 said that . . . windows of his flat he could
see 10 said she'd no idea what the time was but she'd dial 11 his
wife had just been made 12 said she'd come with me . . . she was
13 said he had . . . that afternoon . . . he hadn't done his homework
14 warned her if she let . . . she would scorch her clothes
15 pointed out I hadn't given him . . . bill was . . . I'd paid him
16 Englishmen made . . . they were 17 she liked men . . . she didn't
like them . . . She preferred . . . men looked silly 18 The report
stated that the new Rolls Royce ran . . . all you could hear was . . .
The Managing Director replied that they'd have 19 said she didn't
know . . . her plums. She supposed (said she supposed) she'd have to
. . . trouble was no one in her family ate 20 explained they liked
working . . . they got 21 that he was . . . and he did all his own
22 told Joan she could keep that one if she liked as he had 23 said
he was going fishing with his mother that afternoon and they were

just going 24 told her she had got my umbrella and that hers was in
her bedroom 25 explained to his client that he knew what they had
said because he had bugged 26 said he'd sit up till she came in but
he hoped she wouldn't 27 told me that if I gave him . . . he'd . . .
for me 28 said she had . . . it didn't seem . . . to her weight 29 said
it was . . . and that he used one of them himself 30 said her new
house was supposed to be . . . but that so far she hadn't seen
31 said that if we answered all the questions . . . we might win
32 said that if he pressed his ear . . . he could hear . . . were saying

Exercise 86 (See note above key to Exercise 80. Where there is no
introductory verb, use '. . . said (that) . . .'))

1 he hadn't been able to get . . . he had lost his key, so he had had to
break 2 the mirror was there . . . he could see himself when he was
dancing 3 told him she had written to him two days before and
wondered why he hadn't 4 if the ground was dry . . . his horse
might win 5 advised me to slow down as there was 6 said that if
Tom wanted . . . he'd better apply 7 they had walked . . . the
previous night . . . protest about their rent. The Minister had been
. . . had promised . . . what he could for them 8 said they should
put traffic lights there, otherwise there'd be 9 told them it was time
they began training for their . . . 10 said to me that if I left . . . I
should be there 11 if it rained that afternoon it would be . . . the
following day 12 told her guest she had meant . . . she had plugged
. . . She was always doing 13 he had been intending . . . the next
day . . . didn't think he'd be 14 told Mrs Smith that Bill should do
. . . he had done very well at the school 15 told her husband she
didn't think his father liked her 16 told her the steak was . . . and
said/added that he was not complaining but was just pointing . . . she
said she wished he'd stop 17 reported that the burglars hadn't been
able . . . had carried it 18 told me that if I saw her father I'd
recognize him . . . He was 19 he had found . . . the day before . . .
was going . . . that afternoon 20 he had got out . . . while he was
standing . . . the gears (had) engaged . . . and the boat had
gone/went 21 says he has done 22 asked if he would like me to go
with him. He said he'd rather go . . . *or*, I offered to go with him, but
he said 23 told me I might take his car if I liked and said he
wouldn't be needing it the next day or the day after that 24 that the
previous day Tom and she had gone/been to look . . . he was
thinking . . . It was rather . . . and had a lovely garden but Tom had
decided . . . was opposite 25 his wife wanted to take . . . he'd rather
she concentrated on their home 26 she didn't know what my father
would say when he saw . . . my puppies had made of the £5 note
27 it was high time I passed my test; she was tired 28 said I wished
she had seen it

Exercise 87 1 asked what had happened 2 asked which . . . (had)
inherited 3 asked who was going 4 asked what would happen

5 asked which team had won   6 asked which team (had) won
7 asked who was playing the following week   8 asked who would be
umpiring   9 asked who wanted   10 asked who had just dropped
11 asked where the . . . office was   12 asked what she should do
with her . . .   13 asked what platform the train left   14 asked when
it arrived   15 asked when the timetable had been changed   16 asked
why the 2.30 had been . . .   17 asked how much a day return cost
18 asked why the price went up   19 asked how he could get
20 asked when they were coming   21 asked if a return . . . was
22 asked if puppies travelled   23 asked if she could bring her dog
. . . with her   24 asked if the train stopped   25 asked if you could
telephone   26 asked if the 2.40 had   27 asked if you could get
28 asked if they brought   29 asked if there were   30 asked if he had

Exercise 88   1 asked what country I came from   2 asked how long
I'd been here   3 asked if I was working   4 asked if I had   5 asked
what I was going to study   6 asked if I had enrolled   7 asked if I
wanted to buy   8 asked if I had seen   9 asked if I played   10 asked
if I would have   11 asked if I had played for my . . .   12 asked if I
was interested   13 asked if I would like   14 asked what I thought

Each of the following will begin: she asked/wanted to know/enquired
15 how long it had been   16 if I liked   17 if he was   18 how many
. . . there were   19 how big the classes were   20 if the classes were
21 what the academic standard was like   22 if parents could visit
23 if there was   24 if they taught   25 what . . . could the children
learn   26 if there was   27 if they acted   28 what . . . plays they had
done   29 what games they played   30 if the fields were   31 if they
were taught   32 if the children could get   33 if the food was good
34 if there was   35 how often it met   36 if our boys had been/were
happy

Exercise 89   (**if** is interchangeable with **whether** except in
conditional sentences.)

1 asked why he was looking   2 asked who had put . . . in his coffee
3 asked which of them knew   4 asked why he had travelled
5 inquired how she could run in high-heeled shoes   6 asked them
what their new house was like   7 asked where he was supposed to
go   8 asked him whose car he had borrowed the previous night
9 asked me what she was/had been wearing when I saw her last
10 asked who owned the revolver   11 asked Mr J. where he had
been the previous night   12 asked the boy what else he had seen
13 asked whether he had done that sort   14 asked her if she could
read   15 inquired whether they had understood what I had said to
them   16 asked the customer if he was being attended to   17 asked
him if he would go . . . the others did   18 asked Mary if she saw
what he saw   19 inquired who had left   20 asked him if he had gone

. . . and if he wanted   21 asked why his house was . . . and whether his father had been   22 asked if he was leaving that day or the following morning   23 asked how far it was and how long it would take   24 asked if he could speak to Mrs Pitt. The *au pair* girl answered that she was afraid she was out and asked if she could take   25 asked the little boy if he was sorry for what he had done   26 asked her if she was going to   27 asked the woman if she would mind if he looked inside her bag   28 asked the student if he would know what to do if someone fell at his feet   29 asked her why she thought it might be   30 asked him if he knew. . .shoes he was wearing weren't

Exercise 90 (The following are possible answers. Other introductory verbs are often possible.)

1 He told her to switch off the TV   2 She told Tom to shut   3 I asked Mary to lend me her pen   4 I warned them not to watch   5 He warned me not to believe everything I heard   6 asked me to fill up the   7 I told them not to hurry   8 warned Mary not to touch the switch   9 ordered the bank clerk to open   10 begged me to do as he said   11 told Peter to help his mother   12 told the children not to make   13 told us to do whatever we liked   14 warned them not to miss their train   15 advised his client to read it before he signed it   16 begged her to sing it again   17 warned us not to put our hands   18 advised him to buy   19 begged him not to drive   20 told the boys not to lean their bicycles against his windows   21 asked her to come with him   22 advised her to cook it   23 warned the lady not to touch   24 told the boys not to argue with him   25 told him to pull as hard as he could   26 ordered the porter to send   27 advised us not to lend   28 told us to make a list of what we wanted   29 told her to look   30 warned the people on the platform to stand clear   31 asked the children to see if they could   32 warned her not to go   33 asked the customer to pay   34 the notice told us to leave the space clear   35 I reminded them to write to their   36 warned her to think well before she answered

Exercise 91 (See note above key to Exercise 90.)

1 told me to get out of his   2 ordered me to climb   3 asked the customer to pay   4 asked her to open her   5 told Mrs P. not to worry but (to) leave it all to him   6 warned him not to use   7 told the taxi-driver to follow the car   8 recommended me to wash   9 urged me to have confidence in him   10 told the lift-man to take him   11 advised the passengers to read   12 told her always to cook. . . and never to use   13 told him not to argue with his   14 reminded me to prune   15 told her to wait for him   16 advised her not to eat . . . and to avoid   17 advised me not to say   18 the notice told/asked people not to ask   19 told her not to forget   20 advised/told me to cross   21 asked him to write to her as often as

he could 22 told him to put his 23 asked the porter to find him
24 told me not to forget my 25 told the children not to go 26 told
his men to search 27 told her not to make 28 told/warned him to
put the gun down as it was loaded

Exercise 92 (See note above key to Exercise 90.)

1 advised us to make . . . our time as we wouldn't get 2 urged the
public not to wait till the following day but to post . . . that day
3 warned them to be . . . and reminded me to drive 4 said he
couldn't open it and told/asked Peter to have 5 told me to go and
get him . . . and to come 6 said someone was coming and told/urged
me to get 7 warned us to give way to . . . the/our right 8 begged
us to send whatever we could spare 9 advised him to wear a wig if
he didn't want to be recognized 10 warned/told them not to bathe
when the red flag was flying 11 told him not to forget/reminded
him to thank . . . when he was saying 12 told me to watch . . . and
not to let it 13 told/advised/warned me not to shelter . . . as the tree
might 14 told me to put the message . . . and throw 15 told me to
read it for myself if I didn't believe what he said 16 reminded me to
use my 17 told her husband not to drive . . . or the baby would
18 begged her to make . . . stronger and said that it had been . . . the
previous night 19 warned us to beware 20 told me to smell it and
asked if I thought it had gone bad 21 told him not to take his coat
off as they were going 22 told her to stand by the window and tell
him if anyone went 23 told his pupil not to move till . . . waved him
on 24 told me not to touch it as I would only make 25 warned him
to be careful as the steps were 26 told/asked the girl to ask her
boss . . . and said that my number was . . . She asked me to repeat
it 27 . . . told him to tell them not to work . . . as if they finished
. . . they wouldn't get 28 The placard warned us to prepare to meet
our doom as the end of the world was at hand 29 The instructor
reminded me to put 30 Keiko asked him to take off his

Exercise 93 1 he invited me to have lunch with him 2 offered
me/her/him a 3 asked if they'd mind not smoking/asked them not to
smoke 4 told her to take the . . . and to shut the door as she went
5 asked me to help her as she couldn't 6 said it was a . . . and
advised me to ask 7 advised me to try to/and get 8 offered to wait
for me/said she'd wait if I liked 9 reminded me to switch off when
I'd finished 10 asked/told me to check the figures for him
11 advised me to apologize 12 asked him to check 13 told me to
sit/said he wished I'd sit . . . asked how I expected him to paint me
when I kept jerking my head 14 advised him to go by train as it
was 15 The notice asked guests not to play 16 asked me to wait
17 strongly advised me to see 18 advised them to plant 19 asked
me to sign 20 asked me to forward . . . while he was 21 The police
asked anyone who has seen the . . . to get in touch with their

nearest   22 warned me not to leave my . . . as our host's dogs might mistake me   23 told me to answer the letter and reminded me to keep   24 asked me to move my car as it was blocking his   25 Mrs Jones asked them to let her know when their . . . came in   26 The coach told the first team to report   27 Tom asked Ann to sew on the button for him. Mary advised him to sew it on himself as buttons . . . usually came off   28 The girl asked me to sit down and said . . ./said that if I sat down the fortune teller would be with me

Exercise 94   1 asked if he could get   2 said she couldn't open . . . Tom offered to do it for her   3 asked the official to translate it 4 wondered if they would ever meet   5 asked if I would be there the next day. I said that I would   6 asked if she could lose . . . the doctor said (that) she couldn't   7 offered me a drink   8 urged us to install   9 asked me to read it   10 asked (me) if she should tell him what had happened   11 asked if I wouldn't like to look   12 said she was going . . . Tom said he was too and offered her a lift/asked if she'd like a lift   13 asked for a sweet/asked if he could have a sweet   14 asked if they could stay   15 asked for the weekend/asked if he could have   16 asked if he could leave   17 asked (him) why he didn't like   18 advised him to take up   19 asked where he should hang his . . . and if it would look   20 asked what I should/was to do if the car wouldn't start   21 asked if I had enough . . . and offered to lend me some   22 asked if he would be able to guide me or if I should bring   23 reminded him to shut   24 asked (her) if she would like to see   25 asked me to peel   26 said that he'd got two tickets and invited me to come/go with him   27 asked if I could use . . . I said (that) I couldn't   28 asked if I'd mind living by myself 29 asked me to pay/asked if I'd mind paying   30 asked why she didn't trust him. She said (that) she never trusted

Exercise 95   (See note above key to Exercise 90.)

1 told me to remember to get . . . when I was *or* reminded me to get, etc. *or* said that when I was at . . . I was to get   2 told/advised me to sit down and put my head between my knees if I felt *or* said that if I felt faint I was to put/should put   3 asked what he was to do/should do with my purse if he found it. I told/asked him to keep it till he saw me   4 told me/asked me to give him a drink if he arrived before she got back *or* said that if he arrived before she got back I was to give   5 told me if anyone rang up to say *or* said that if anyone rang up I was to say she'd be   6 told me when I was driving always to look in my mirror *or* said that when I was driving I should always look   7 told me to leave the key under the mat if I went out *or* said that if I went out I was to leave   8 told me to shut the window if I thought the room was cold *or* said that if I thought the room was cold I was to shut/should shut   9 told me to ring him up if I felt lonely any time *or* said that if I felt lonely I was to ring   10 said that

if she didn't eat meat I was to offer her an omelette (*the* **tell** *construction would be very clumsy here*)   11 told me to get the car off the road if I had a puncture and not to leave *or* said that if I had a puncture I was to get/should get . . . and not leave   12 told me to take the letter to the police if he wasn't back by that time the next day *or* said that if he wasn't back by . . . I was to take   13 told her husband not to forget/reminded him to thank Mrs Pitt when he saw her   14 told me to take the meat out of the oven when the bell rang *or* said that when the bell rang I was to take/should take   15 told them to give their . . . if they were taken . . . but to refuse to answer *or* said that if they were taken . . . they were to give . . . but (to) refuse   16 told them to shut . . . and go . . . when they heard *or* said that when they heard . . . they were to shut . . . and go   17 told me to press . . . if the lift should stop/stopped *or* said that if the lift should stop/stopped . . . I was to press/should press   18 told me to ask a client if he had a weak heart before I allowed him *or* said that before I allowed anyone . . . I was to ask/should ask   19 asked what she should/was to say if the police stopped her   20 asked what she should do if he refused to let her in. I told her to write   21 asked/wondered what would happen if the strike continued   22 . . .how they would get food if it went on   23 . . . asked if they could go . . . the rain stopped   24 said that when they'd . . . they were to   25 advised her to switch . . . if she didn't like   26 asked whether/if the bank would repay . . . if I lost   27 told me I had/'d better complain . . . if the noise got   28 said I was to ring him and give him . . . as soon as I found

Exercise 96   Part 1 (Alternative constructions are often possible.)

1–14 Ann suggested having a party on the following Saturday. Mary agreed and asked who they should invite. Ann was against making a list and suggested they should just invite everybody. Mary said they didn't want to do much cooking and proposed making it a wine and cheese party. Ann then suggested that they should ask everyone to bring a bottle. Mary reminded her that they hadn't many glasses left and suggested hiring glasses from their local wineshop. Ann suggested having the party in the garden if it was warm and then Mary put forward the idea of a barbecue. Ann thought this was a good idea and said they could ask Paul to do the cooking. Mary remembered that last time they had had a barbecue the neighbours had complained about the noise, and she wondered if they should ask everyone to speak in whispers. Ann suggested going round to the neighbours instead and apologizing in advance. Mary, however, proposed inviting the neighbours, adding that then the noise wouldn't matter. Ann thought that was a clever idea and suggested ringing everyone up that night, but Mary prudently suggested working out how much it would cost first.

Part 2   15 Mrs Smith suggested . . . but her husband suggested renting . . ., adding that it was all they could afford. 16 I suggested that Ann should complain, saying that the boss was more likely to listen to her 17 She reminded him that he used to be . . . and suggested that he should 18 He proposed walking . . . as it was not far and I agreed 19 Ann suggested (our) joining a weaving class, adding that there was one 20 The children suggested organizing . . . the teacher proposed 21 I asked Bill where we should meet and he suggested the hotel 22 I suggested to Ann that she should ring him and ask him what he thought 23 I pointed out I was doing . . . and suggested that he should give me/him giving me 24 He proposed leaving/that they should leave adding that he hated 25 Their father suggested that the children should go 26 I suggested his/him asking them what they would like to do 27 He suggested that we should begin training . . . I said I had . . . and suggested that he should ask Paul 28 They suggested me/my putting an advertisement in the local paper.

Exercise 97 (The following are possible answers only.)

1 warned us not to walk on the ice as it wasn't 2 introduced Miss White to Miss Brown 3 gave/handed her the keys, advising/and advised her to wait 4 begged me not to tell . . . I promised not to/promised (that) I wouldn't 5 offered him my torch but he refused as/explaining that he had one of his own 6 Tom offered to pay. Ann protested but he insisted. 7 invited us to come in and look round, assuring us that there was no 8 threatened to kill the boy if they didn't pay 9 refused to answer any questions 10 complained that he expected . . . agreed (with her) 11 wished it would 12 pointed out that I had pressed . . . He warned me not to do . . . I might have 13 exclaimed that her weight had gone up . . . she admitted/agreed that it had 14 hoped I'd have a good journey/wished me a good journey and reminded me to send a card when I arrived 15 exclaimed with delight that he had passed . . . I congratulated him and wished him luck 16 She agreed to wait 17 wished him many happy returns of his . . . and he thanked us 18 pointed out/remarked that my door was . . . I agreed (with her)/I admitted it 19 He offered me a cigarette and I accepted 20 Their mother threatened to sell . . . if they kept . . . The children begged her not to do that, promising not to quarrel/assuring her that they wouldn't quarrel 21 offered me £500 to keep my 22 He promised to wait for me 23 I apologized for being late and explained that the bus had broken 24 accused him of leaking . . . He denied it. Tom called him a liar. 25 threatened to drop us from the team if we did not train 26 complained that if the boys did . . . he called them his sons, but that if they did . . . he called them hers. 27 Tom suggested having a rest and Ann agreed. 30 He exclaimed with disgust that there was a slug in his . . . and called

Key

Exercise 98 (Other alternatives are possible here.)

1 Tom: Would you like to come for a drive, tomorrow, Ann?
2 Ann: I'd love to. Where are you thinking of going, Tom?
3 Tom: Well, I'll leave it to you.
4 Ann: What about Stratford?
5 I haven't been there for ages.
6 Tom: Good idea!/All right. We might go on the river if it's a fine day.
7 Ann: I wonder what's on at the Royal Shakespeare Theatre.
8 Tom: We'll find out when we get there.
9 It's usually possible to get seats on the day of the play.
10 Can you be ready by ten?
11 Ann: I'm afraid not, Tom/I'm very sorry, Tom, but I can't. I have to type a report first.
12 Tom: Working on Saturday! What a horrible idea!
13 I'd change my job if I were you.
14 Ann: Don't be ridiculous, Tom!
15 I volunteered to type the report in return for a free afternoon next week.
16 I didn't know you were going to ask me out, after all.
17 Tom: Oh well, I suppose it's all right.
18 But don't make a habit of volunteering for weekend work, will you?
19 Ann: No, I promise I won't.
20 Tom: (gloomily) I suppose you'll be busy all morning.
21 Ann: No, no! I'll be finished by 11.00.
22 Shall I meet you at the bus stop at Hyde Park Corner?
23 Tom: That isn't a very good meeting place. I'll call for you.
24 Ann: That's very good of you, Tom. I'll be waiting in the hall.
25 Tom: Let's climb to the top. The view from there is marvellous.
26 Ann: But we've been climbing for three hours already. I'm too tired to go any further.
27 Why don't you go on up? I'll go down and wait there.
28 Tom: All right. Here are the car keys. You'd better wait in the car./You could wait in the car, couldn't you?
29 I'll be as quick as I can.
30 Ann: There'll be no lunch left if you're too long. I'll have eaten it all!

10 Purpose

Exercise 99 (so as is interchangeable with in order.)

1 to paint 2 to remind 3 to feed 4 so as not to frighten 5 to put his savings in 6 to drink out of 7 to save 8 so as not to strain 9 in order to get 10 to tell 11 so as not to get 12 to frighten 13 so as not to make 14 to protect 15 to put on the fire 16 so as

not to disturb   17 to study   18 in order to discuss   19 so as to be
able   20 to elude   21 to prevent   22 to reduce   23 (in order) to
read   24 to watch   25 in order to have   26 in order to keep   27 (in
order) to learn   28 to buy   29 to warn   30 to avoid   31 to protect
32 so as to be able   33 to warn   34 to avoid   35 (in order) to look
36 so as not to alarm

Exercise 100   (**I/we would** is replaceable by **I/we should.**
would/wouldn't in negative purpose clauses is usually replaceable by
should/shouldn't. Where an infinitive phrase is possible the infinitive
given in the key is not necessarily the only one that could be used.
To save space not more than two possible answers are given for any
one example. Sometimes the **in case** construction would also be
possible. **in case** can be followed by **should** + infinitive, though an
ordinary present or past tense is more usual.)

1 so that nobody should/would know *or* to prevent anyone knowing
2 in case somebody knocks   3 so that repair work may/can continue
or to allow repair work to continue   4 so that it wouldn't get broken
or to prevent it getting broken   5 so that he wouldn't be recognized
or to avoid being recognized   6 so that her fruit wouldn't be stolen
or to prevent her fruit being stolen   7 so that I wouldn't overhear *or*
to prevent my overhearing   8 in case you get bitten   9 so that the
crew may/can escape *or* to enable the crew to escape   10 so that my
children may/will have   11 so that the cows won't get *or* to prevent
the cows getting   12 so that the call wouldn't be *or* to prevent the
call being   13 so that the birds won't eat *or* to prevent the birds
eating   14 in case there is   15 so that nobody will/can climb *or* to
prevent anyone climbing   16 in case you have   17 so that the snow
would/could slide   18 so that everyone may/will understand *or* to
enable everyone to understand   19 so that anyone who finds him
will/may know   20 so that the birds would know *or* to let the birds
know   21 in case we are   22 so that the birds won't build *or* to
prevent the birds building   23 in case he forgets   24 so that she
wouldn't frighten *or* to prevent her frightening   25 in case the
chimney catches   26 so that I couldn't/wouldn't be able to call *or* to
prevent me calling   27 in case it is   28 so that young children won't
be able to turn *or* to prevent young children turning   29 in case he
breaks   30 so that the government may/can discuss *or* to let the
government discuss   31 in case it is   32 so that pedestrians
might/could cross *or* to let pedestrians cross   33 so that his secretary
could/would be able to   34 in case they set   35 so that the rest of
the party would know *or* to let the rest of the party know   36 so that
the meat won't burn *or* to prevent the meat burning *or* in case the
meat burns